HISTORICAL NOTES

ON

ST. BENEDICT'S "RULE FOR MONKS"

BY

ILDEPHONSE CARDINAL SCHUSTER, *O.S.B.*

Translated by

LEONARD J. DOYLE

THE SHOE STRING PRESS, INC.

HAMDEN, CONNECTICUT

1962

IMPRIMATUR:

St. Cloud, Minnesota, May 24, 1961

✠ *Peter W. Bartholome*
Bishop

Library of Congress Catalog Card No. 61-18384
Printed in the United States of America

CONTENTS

HISTORICAL NOTES

ON

ST. BENEDICT'S "RULE FOR MONKS"

PREFACE

In 1880, the year I was born, the Catholic world under the auspices of the great Leo XIII was celebrating the fourteenth centenary of the birth of St. Benedict, patriarch of Western monachism.

In 1947, when the centenary of his death will be celebrated, either I shall no longer be here or I shall no longer be able to write books.* As a loyal son, therefore, I wanted to offer my contribution to the Saint in anticipation, by publishing these historical notes now. If the tradition which was current during my youth, that St. Benedict was born in 480 and died in 540, had not later been refuted by history, I would undoubtedly have opened the centenary festivities with this publication of mine.

I have called these pages simply historical notes, because that is all they are. The definitive historical monument on St. Benedict will always remain the second book of the Dialogs of St. Gregory, together with the Rule for Monks. But these two primary sources are a good fourteen centuries distant from us, so that, in order to understand them without running into anachronisms, we must project the scene against the background of the Roman world in the first half of the sixth century.

St. Gregory for the most part could abstract from that back-

*Translator's note: This prediction was happily wrong. Before his death in 1954, Cardinal Schuster had written a complete commentary on the Rule, which I have permission to translate; a thorough biography, St. Benedict and His Times, translated by the Rev. Gregory J. Roettger, O.S.B. (St. Louis: B. Herder Book Co., 1951); and a daily thought on the Rule of St. Benedict for the liturgical year.

ground, since he was writing for a public quite familiar with those realities. For us, on the contrary, the reconstruction of the historical and juridical conditions of St. Benedict's work is much more laborious.

I have attempted to excavate and labor in this field. If I am not deceiving myself, the historical figure of the holy Patriarch stands out more vivid and more true, and the Benedictine code acquires a greater light and authority from the fact illustrated in these notes that the unification of monastic discipline by means of the Rule for Monks must undoubtedly have been initiated and completed under the auspices of the Roman pontificate.

In the sixth century the only one who was able to promulgate a Holy Rule or general laws for monasteries was the Pope for the whole Church or the metropolitan bishop for his province. St. Benedict, therefore, with his sanctity, his insight, his experience, drew up the desired code, and the Holy See then approved it and diffused it throughout the Latin world.

I have attempted to throw some light on St. Benedict's monastic apostolate in the Simbruini valley, and then on the missionary apostolate in the transformation of the Cassinese temples and the conversion of those in the vicinity from idolatry to the Christian faith. By properly fitting the Gregorian terminology and the episodes of this evangelizing work of the Patriarch into the canonical discipline of the time, we gain some insight also into his priestly action on the people whom he first converted and then arranged into parishes, and of whom he kept the supervisory direction.

Having arrived here at the end of my studies and of my life, I can better understand how, almost at once after St. Benedict's death, the monachism formed according to his spiritual doctrine branched out generously in all directions throughout the fields of

4

the Catholic apostolate: set out for the distant missions, instituted schools and hospitals, tilled the soil and improved whole regions, prepared Pontiffs and Doctors for the Church. Not one of those engaged in this evangelical work ever thought of leaving the royal way marked out by St. Benedict.

Throughout the Middle Ages Benedictine monachism — the Benedictine order is a juridical concept developed somewhat later — fulfilled alone that whole manifold apostolate of good to which today's numerous religious families attend, each in its own field and according to its own vocation.

All those various purposes and particular vocations, Benedictine monachism beautifully and effectively united and included in one unique higher spirit which makes the monk "the workman of God". St. Benedict several times uses this glorious title for the monk, just as the Romans later will call their bishop St. Gregory "the consul of God". Both he and they intended to say, therefore, that the monk, consecrating himself to the divine service in the field of the Church, puts himself at the free disposal of the Master for all those labors which may fall to him. Although the work may vary with the variations in station, what remains unchanged and unchangeable is "the holy service they have professed" (Rule of St. Benedict, ch. 5). This is precisely the characteristic which the ancient Christians perceived in the monk when they gave him the title "servant of God", leaving to Gregory the Great the privilege later on of entitling himself "the last of all the monks", that is "the servant of the servants of God".

But in St. Benedict's conception this "holy service", rather than being merely performed, must be perpetually lived in community, in a definite religious family: "serving under a Rule and an abbot". St. Benedict directs himself exclusively to the cenobites: "to lay down a Rule for the strongest kind, the cenobites" (Rule, ch. 1).

The later concept of the guardian, rector or superior named periodically by the provincial chapter is not at all adapted to the Benedictine ideal, which conceives of the abbey as an advanced school of high spirituality or as a "house of God", whose patriarchal government is founded altogether on the paternal and educative authority of the "father" or "abbot".

To these primary elements of the Benedictine life must be added the "Work of God" or the principal "service of their devotion" (Rule, ch. 18), which is choral prayer at fixed hours.

These fundamental canons of Benedictine monachism were generally kept intact during the Middle Ages. For the rest, it was an easy adaptation of the "workmen of God" to the various historical or regional climates which suggested this or that kind of sacred activity in service of the Church.

These last words must be emphasized. I speak of sacred activity, because it was done by the monks in the name of that "holy service they have professed". I speak likewise of the "service of the Church"; for in the Middle Ages Benedictine monachism, not having any religious order to promote because there was none as yet, promoted instead the good of the Catholic Church and the reign of God in souls.

Practically all the ancient pontifical privileges generously granted the various abbeys are reducible to this: to safeguard with papal authority the tranquil observance in monasteries of the Rule for Monks without conflict with any other jurisdiction.

Without being very old, still I have lived long enough to know several monastic personalities who in the second half of the nineteenth century distinguished themselves by the singular holiness of their lives and the great benefits they bestowed on the Catholic family: Cardinal Dusmet, Abbot Zelli, Abbot Placidus Wolter, Msgr. Rudesind Salvado, the servant of God Placidus Riccardi, and others.

These personages lived in very different external conditions, imposed by the difficult circumstances of the times. And yet they revealed an identical spirit: Msgr. Salvado in the woods of New Norcia among the cannibals, as well as Dom Placidus among the woods which surround the desolate abbey of Farfa, revealed that same austere and total dedication to God "because of the holy service they professed" which in the case of Cardinal Dusmet converted the archiepiscopal palace of Catania into a sort of monastery. For these "great spirits" the real cloister, in place of the material cloister, was they themselves, with the community life organized by them in diligent, constant prayer and work for holy Church.

I am ever more convinced of the fertility of the Benedictine institute, and I think it has not yet written the last chapters of its history. The more refined spirituality of many souls today keeps turning more and more towards the liturgical prayer of the Church and the most ancient sources of the spiritual life. After so many disillusionments in the many different social fields, today there is a numerous group of souls who feel something like a homesickness for the divine and a need of seeking God according to the authentic forms of the Church. If this movement, now in its beginnings, continues to grow, St. Benedict will still have a decisive word to say to a future generation of seekers of God ("whether he is truly seeking God" — Rule, ch. 58). If this word is listened to, an ancient apocryphal oracle which was said to have been made by divine revelation to the Patriarch of Western monachism will be verified in an unexpected way:

7

Your order shall stand to the very end, and in the last days it shall be a most faithful mainstay of the Roman Church.

Milan, on the feast of St. Benedict, March 21, 1940.

Ildephonse, Cardinal Archbishop

Monastic Legislation

"With all the renown he gained by his numerous miracles",
writes St. Gregory the Great, "the holy man was no less outstand-
ing for the wisdom of his teaching. He wrote a <u>Rule for Monks</u> that
is remarkable for its discretion and its clarity of language. Anyone
who wishes to know more about his life and character can discover
in his Rule exactly what he was like as an abbot, for his life could
not have differed from his teaching" (<u>Dialogs</u>, book 2, ch. 36).

The Cassinese Colony in the Lateran

Above is the most ancient and authoritative document about the
<u>Rule</u> of St. Benedict. While Gregory was writing these sentences,
the manuscript in the Saint's own hand was being placed into the
archives of the Lateran palace, where the originals of the more important documents of the Roman Church were preserved. It had
been brought there about 589 by St. Benedict's disciples in their
flight from Monte Cassino. The Lombard armies of Zotto of Bene-
vento had invaded the place at night, leaving the edifice a desolate
ruin but fortunately sparing its inhabitants, in accordance with the
divine promise to the holy Patriarch. Pope Pelagius I had welcomed
the refugees, sheltering them in the Lateran monastery.

In the counsels of divine Providence it was written, therefore,
that this misfortune should be converted into a favorable and decisive circumstance, which would have an influence on the future
destiny of Western monachism.

We learn from history, in fact, that the Cassinese sojourn in the Lateran and the deposit of the autograph of the Rule in the pontifical archives had the effect of conferring something like a seal of the Roman pontificate on the Benedictine institute. Without the emigration to Rome and the intervention of the papacy, St. Benedict's disciples might easily have remained just another community of cenobites. Instead, at Rome and in the shadow of the papal residence they became the precious seed, as it were, of a new, Latin monasticism, which in the name of the papacy continued to diffuse itself throughout the world as a ferment of evangelical perfection within the Roman unity.

The Autograph Manuscript of the "Rule"

Unfortunately, we have too few documents on the external history of that autograph manuscript of St. Benedict deposited in the papal scrinium. The tradition of Monte Cassino relates that in the nocturnal flight with Zotto's swords at their throats, the disciples of the great Patriarch did abandon monastery, furniture and all the rest, but together with their lives thought to bring to safety the sacred relics of their Father, that is: the manuscript of the Rule; the bronze weight of bread used by him for each monk's daily ration; and finally one of the original two hundred sacks which, during the scarcity of the year 536, divine Providence had miraculously caused to be found, filled with flour, at the gates of Monte Cassino.

About a hundred and fifty years later, those sacred keepsakes were restored to the monks by Pope Zachary, when Abbot Petronax had led back a colony of monks to repopulate the ancient monastery of St. Benedict.[1]

From certain inelegant verses prefixed to the Benedictine Rule at the time of Simplicius, the Patriarch's second successor in the government of Monte Cassino, we are informed that until then the Master's manuscript had remained almost unknown in the cupboards of the archives. It was Simplicius himself who brought it to light, taking care of its diffusion through Rome. There is no reason for disbelieving the ingenuous testimony of this obscure Cassinese poet, who showed himself so primitive and naïve as to evaluate equally the merits of the holy Lawgiver and those of his posthumous editor: "Yet one reward remains to both forever."[2]

Notwithstanding the fact that the Cassinese tradition defers the foundation of the Lateran monastery until the time of Abbot Bonitus and of the emigration to Rome in 589, I have always maintained doubts on this late chronology, somewhat adapted by Paul the Deacon.

Writing his Dialogs during 593 and 594, St. Gregory said of Abbot Valentinian, already deceased, that he was "for many years superior of the monastery at the Lateran". To determine just when these "many years" were, we must set back the beginning of his abbacy at least twenty-five years, that is to the time when Constantine, St. Benedict's immediate successor, was presiding at Monte Cassino.

When St. Gregory was dictating the Dialogs, about 594, it was a fact already belonging to history that the administration of Valentinian in the Lateran monastery had lasted a long time and was now a mere historical remembrance. Gregory had known him well, as before him he had known Abbot Constantine, "a very venerable man", and after Valentinian he had connections with Abbot Simplicius, successor of Constantine.

The fact that Gregory inserts the long Lateran abbacy of Valentinian between the Cassinese administrations of Constantine and Simplicius seems to confirm the hypothesis that well before the invasion by Duke Zotto the disciples of St. Benedict had made some separation in their community in order to go and serve the beautiful Lateran basilica. We are on the very morrow of St. Benedict's death, therefore, and already Valentinian and his monks are entering into relations with the Holy See and becoming established near the pontifical residence itself.

Gregory at that time was still young, and with his pious mother Sylvia he lived on the nearby Clivus Scauri, on the Caelian hill. His location helps to explain his assiduous and long relations with the various abbots of Monte Cassino, Rome and Subiaco and his spiritual colloquies with the immediate disciples of the Patriarch St. Benedict. I could go further, observing that the description of the Cassinese monastery's topography in St. Gregory is so precise as to reveal the mind and the pen of one who had known those places familiarly and well, even in the least topographical details.

After 574 Gregory I abandoned the honors of the pretura urbana to transform his own palace on the Caelian hill into a monastery, where for the first time he made profession of the monastic life. We should not fail to observe that the Rule of St. Benedict served as the monastic code for the new community.

Abbot Valentinian at that time was already governing the "Lateran monastery"; and, considering the close relations of St. Gregory's family with those first disciples of St. Benedict at Rome, it is easy to infer the influence exercised by St. Benedict's disciples on the new foundation in the old papal residence.

The question remains unsolved as to when the monastery at the Lateran was properly founded. The chronological data furnished by St. Gregory impel us decisively towards the middle of the sixth century; beyond that nothing but hypotheses can be made.

When St. Benedict was ending his days at Monte Cassino, not

before 547, Pope Vigilius was living as a prisoner at Constantinople. He died there after an absence of ten years, and his body was brought back to Rome. It is hard to suppose that during those unhappy years the priest Mareas, the Pope's vicar at Rome, could have dared to found a monastery right next to the Lateran episcopal residence.

In 556 Pelagius I succeeded to the papacy. His first years were so disturbed by the schism of the Three Chapters that it is not too easy for the historian to insert the Benedictine foundation at the Lateran into the biography of that Pontiff, who at the time was thought to have caused the death of Pope Silverius and to have betrayed his faith. The historian thinks rather of Popes Agapitus or Silverius, from whom in all probability St. Benedict received the commission to draw up the Rule and to attend to the conversion of the Cassinese people to the Christian faith.

From an ancient inscription referred to in the Sillogi we know that the house of Pope Agapitus on the Caelian was next to that of the parents of Gregory the Great. Right there this great Pope Gregory thought out and composed the work of the Dialogs, including the biography of St. Benedict. This connection perhaps is not accidental. Just as Agapitus I at the suggestion of Cassiodorus fostered the project of a kind of higher biblical school in Rome, so he may have courted the idea of the unification of monastic discipline by means of the official drafting of a single Rule.

In those years the example of Caesarius of Arles and his constant relations with the Lateran court must have had such influence on the minds of his contemporaries that St. Benedict, as we shall see later, actually planned his work on the scheme of the metropolitan of Arles. Caesarius died August 27, 543, when perhaps St. Benedict had already started drawing up the Rule.

13

The foundation of the "Lateran monastery" at the middle of the sixth century, therefore, might be pushed a little ahead to bring Agapitus and Caesarius into the picture. Then it would be easier to explain how the Patriarch of monasticism may have received directly from the Pope the commission to prepare for Italy and for the Lateran a Rule for Monks, just as the metropolitan of Arles had already done for his province.

I have mentioned Cassiodorus, who, with the approval of Pope Agapitus, wanted to institute at Rome a sort of higher school of scriptural studies. We read also of a library which at one time Cassiodorus fears may have been ruined by Totila's army when it occupied Rome in December, 546.

At any rate, his first intention having gone unfulfilled, in about 540, when he was already advanced in years, Theodoric's minister, having arrived at the height of fame and power, suddenly abandoned his office and the world and retired into Calabria to Vivarium. There he founded a double monastery, which he governed until he was more than 90 years old.

What motive could have induced Cassiodorus at the age of 60 to abandon politics and embrace the monastic state? The historians usually explain such a late vocation by observing that the statesman of the kingdom of the Goths, disillusioned with human affairs, now saw no salvation for the remains of ancient letters and civilization except in the consolidation of the monastic state and in the scientific organization of the monasteries.

Between 535 and 536 he had attempted the foundation of the biblical institute at Rome. There, however, he had encountered difficulties. And so after 540 he takes up his design again and completes it at Vivarium, where he founds both school and library, this time by means of his monks.

There is no way of discovering any certain relation between St. Benedict and Cassiodorus. It is important, however, to notice that the personages most representative of the epoch felt deeply the problem of the organization of the monastic life in Italy, and had recourse to the Pope, with a view to the mission of preserving literature and civilization in the Noah's-ark of the monasteries.

It is amazing how much the aged Cassiodorus did at Vivarium to assemble and form a library which included the whole scope of the arts and sciences of that time. Anyone who would like to get an idea of the library of which St. Benedict speaks in the Rule (ch. 48 and 49) should study the one at Vivarium, as Cassiodorus himself describes it in An Introduction to Divine and Human Readings.

Besides, the topographical plan of the "monastic town" as St. Benedict conceives it (Rule, ch. 66) finds its counterpart in the monastery of Vivarium. It is interesting, however, to observe that, with the copious and varied literary production of Cassiodorus for his monks, still he did not write nor impose on them a Rule. Why? It would not have been a work within his competence.

* * *

To prescind from the questions discussed by the various critical editors concerning the history of the text of the Rule and its first two or three drafts by the labor of St. Benedict, of Simplicius or of others, the very succession of chapters seems to point to something like a fusion, not altogether successful, of two drafts of the monastic code.

Let the following parallel series of chapters, for example, be compared with each other:

(Ch. 2). "What Kind of Man the Abbot Ought to Be".	(Ch. 64). "On Constituting an Abbot".
(Ch. 5). "The first degree of humility is obedience without delay."	(Ch. 7). "The first degree of humility is that a person keep the fear of God ever before his eyes."
(Ch. 19). "On the Manner of Saying the Divine Office".	(Ch. 20). "On Reverence in Prayer".
(Ch. 21). "On the Deans of the Monastery".	(Ch. 65). "On the Prior of the Monastery", in which the Saint insists on his original idea of substituting deans for the office of prior, which he held to be too dangerous. He adjusts to the latter, however, in spite of himself, when the circumstances of the environment demand it.
Benedictine "Penitential" No. 1, comprised in ch. 23-30.	"Penitential" No. 2, comprised in ch. 43-46.
(Ch. 53). ". . . Let there be a separate kitchen for the abbot", etc.	(Ch. 56). "Concerning the Abbot's Table".
Compare ch. 60. "On Priests Who May Wish to Live in the Monastery".	(Ch. 62). "On the Priests of the Monastery".
(Ch. 66. Epilogue). "We desire that this Rule be read often in the community, so that none of the brethren may excuse himself on the ground	(Ch. 73, that is, after six more chapters. Epilogue). ". . . whoever you are, therefore, who are hastening to the heavenly homeland, fulfil with the help of

of ignorance."   Christ this minimum Rule which
                                  we have written for beginners
                                  . . ."

These duplications found in the Holy Rule are quite numerous.
They give us the impression of having been originally spread out
over separate sheets of paper or parchment, without a really definite order as yet. The author kept working at his task a little at a
time, but perhaps never brought it to completion. When Abbot Simplicius finally gathered the sheets into one volume, he did not want
to suppress anything of what St. Benedict had written at different
times. Out of this came the present Cassinese recension of the
Rule; while outside of Italy some prior text, perhaps consigned by
St. Benedict to one of the disciples sent far away, was following its
own way and its own fortune.

One could go still further, even to discovering some indication
in the Benedictine Rule of modifications of ideas or penalties, which
the author would not have had time to eliminate from the final text.

In chapter 21, for example, "On the Deans of the Monastery",
the community is divided into deaneries, rather than being commit-
ted solely to the vigilance of a prior, who could easily have created
opposition to the abbot. The more strongly St. Benedict pronounces
himself against the institution of priors who make a counterpoise
to the abbot, the more he fosters the system of deans, each presiding over no more than ten or a dozen religious.

Nevertheless, the tradition of priors in Italy was stronger than
the disparagement of St. Benedict, and it prevailed. The Cassinese
Lawgiver himself has something like a presentiment of this, so that
he has to modify the Rule in two distinct chapters (21 and 65) to
make allowance for the prior.

The recent studies on the relations between the Rule of St. Benedict and the one called the Rule of the Master have permitted the hypothesis that the author of the latter may have used a text of the Benedictine Rule anterior to the one edited by Simplicius. This text must have ended at chapter 66 with the words of the epilogue still preserved: "We desire that this Rule be read often in the community, so that none of the brethren may excuse himself on the ground of ignorance." The quotations from Cassian are much more faithful and literal than in the Cassinese text. There, instead, the hand of the author is easily seen as he polishes his work and renders it clearer and more translucent.

In Search of the Lawgiver

But besides the investigations on the various drafts of the Benedictine code, there is another most important circumstance which must be noticed in the Rule.

Except for St. Pachomius in Egypt, no one before St. Benedict had drawn up a monastic code in the West without having derived the authority for it from the episcopal office. To promulgate a law for persons consecrated to God, falling in the category of ecclesiastics, was considered at that time as an act of authority eminently papal or episcopal, neither more nor less so than the various conciliar statutes regarding consecrated virgins.

This point is exemplified in the lives of St. Basil, St. Ambrose and St. Augustine, and above all in the work of St. Caesarius of Arles. St. Caesarius was St. Benedict's contemporary, and for that reason his work became one of the sources or outlines of the Rule for Monks.

That an authority less than that of a bishop should dictate a Rule for Monks not merely for his own monastery but in general for the various monasteries; that, moreover, he should entitle it <u>Holy</u> and <u>Master</u>; that he should attribute to it an absolute authority to direct the monastic life for monks and for abbots, so as to qualify as "rash" any deviation from it — this is a thing so foreign to the juridical conditions of the sixth century that no one would ever have tolerated it in a person who had not been endowed with episcopal or pontifical power.

And yet the <u>Rule</u> of St. Benedict was drawn up in these precise conditions and with the declared aim of being not just a manual of ascetic life or the Rule of Monte Cassino, but a true law of universal character, in brief the <u>Rule for Monks</u>.

Who conferred this legislative authority on St. Benedict, and why? This is the problem that calls for solution.

It is well to mention that before St. Benedict's time, in the absence of a real monastic code for the numerous monasteries of Italy, there were other norms: the ecclesiastical canons, the imperial legislation and the living teaching of the abbot, inspired by the tradition of the holy Fathers, which was kept in practice by the communities.

At Monte Cassino also, the situation must have been much the same if until the time of Abbot Simplicius the Patriarch's code remained still unpublished, "the hidden work of the Master".

This oral instruction and spiritual direction on the part of the abbots in the sixth century gave rise, however, to many dangers, such as the danger that with the succession of superiors the instruction might become too oscillating and changeable, to the detriment of regularity in the monasteries.

At Arles St. Caesarius, in his capacity as metropolitan of the district, had been the first to dictate a common Rule and impose it on all the male communities dependent on him. "Here begins in the name of Christ the Rule, as it ought to be in a monastery where there is an abbot, whoever he be."

From the title which precedes the Rule we know that the saintly bishop transmitted it to the various monasteries subject to him, that it might be observed without fail: "Transmitted by St. Tetradius, priest, nephew of St. Caesarius of blessed memory, bishop of Arles and abbot, at the request of my lowly person; and said by Tetradius to have been dictated by his lord, the above-mentioned Caesarius; and transmitted by Caesarius to the various monasteries during his episcopate."[3]

The episcopacy, which already had authority over the monasteries as places consecrated to the service of God, was finally taking directly in hand the spiritual formation and the very discipline of the monks, just as it had already done for the virgins consecrated to God.

But St. Caesarius was too great a bishop not to understand that for complete stability and authority his legislative work for the monasteries of monks and nuns of his metropolitan province needed above all the confirmation and sanction of the apostolic See.

It was in the character and custom of the holy pontiff of Arles always to cover his theological or pastoral initiatives with the mantle of the Holy See. Seven Popes succeeded one another during his episcopate, and from each one Caesarius knew how to obtain privileges, decrees, theological or canonical decisions, which opportunely went to strengthen his authority as metropolitan, or rather his assignment as vicar of the Holy See for Gaul.

Caesarius did the same for his monastic institutions. He wrote two distinct Rules, one for monks and one for nuns, and finally a Recapitulation to determine once and for all the essential points of the Rule for Virgins. The affinity of these Rules with that of St.

20

Benedict has already been established by various authors.

In the Recapitulation the author tells the history of those Rules: he would write one page today, add another chapter tomorrow, modify one passage another day, revise another the next day; it had turned out to be like a body without cohesion or fusion. "Many times afterward, however, we added something to it or took something away." What does the bishop do in the end? He gathers all that material into summary chapters in the Recapitulation or final recension, annulling the preceding notes: "And for that reason we wish whatever notes we made previously to be void."

To assure after his death the future of his monastery of St. John for virgins, erected near the ramparts of Arles, Caesarius has recourse to Pope Hormisdas, who in approving his foundation praises the bishop for having given so great an impulse to the monastic life both among men and among women.

All this was happening at the very time when St. Benedict at Subiaco and at Monte Cassino was attending to an identical enterprise!

If the metropolitan of Arles, who was moreover papal vicar in Gaul, felt the need of having his monastic statutes fortified with the papal seal, one may well imagine that this identical need was felt more strongly by St. Benedict, who, both through his numerous monastic churches and through his missionary activity among the pagans of the Campania, must necessarily have entered into frequent relations with the civil and religious powers of the region.

* * *

Accustomed as we are to the present juridical condition of the regulars, dependent directly on the Holy See through the medium of their own superiors, we sometimes conceive and reconstruct the ancient world on our twentieth century ideas.

St. Benedict was rich in sanctity, in wisdom, in charismatic gifts, almost certainly invested with the dignity of the priesthood, with the charge of exercising that sacerdotal dignity in the Cassinese region which we had converted to the faith. Still he lacked one thing that would enable him to promulgate a code or Rule for Monks: the ecclesiastical lawmaking power, which resided, as the case might be, in the metropolitan bishop or in the Roman Pontiff.

The truly universal character of the Benedictine code supposes an equally universal authority which promulgates and imposes it. That is why I have thought of the various Popes who could have been in contact with St. Benedict: of Pope Symmachus; of Hormisdas, who was from Frosinone, not far from Monte Cassino; of Felix IV, ancestor of St. Gregory the Great, the future biographer of St. Benedict; of Silverius; of Vigilius; and above all of Agapitus.

* * *

The better to understand the origins of the Benedictine Rule, it is helpful to have before our eyes that of St. Caesarius of Arles, on which it seems to have been traced. Caesarius legislates above all in his role of metropolitan, and imposes the observance of his law on all the monasteries subject to his archiepiscopal jurisdiction.

He begins, as does St. Benedict, with determining what qualities the abbot ought to possess. But a comparison between the two Rules is opportune.

ST. CAESARIUS	ST. BENEDICT
"Here begins in the name of Christ the Rule. What kind of man an abbot should be in the monastery where he is, whoever he be.*	"What Kind of Man the Abbot Ought to Be" (ch. 2).
"In the first place, if anyone comes for the reformation of his life, let him be received on the condition that he persevere there until his death" (n. 1).	"When anyone is newly come for the reformation of his life . . . he shall make a promise of his stability" (ch. 58). ". . . persevering in the monastery according to His teaching until death" (prol.)
No one could be received into a monastery "unless he first makes a bill of sale of his property" in favor either of his parents or of the monastery. "Let him reserve nothing for himself."	"If he has any property, let let him either give it beforehand to the poor or by solemn donation bestow it on the monastery, reserving nothing at all for himself" (ch. 58).

*Translator's note: The text and punctuation as given here by Cardinal Schuster are: Incipit in Christi nomine Regula. Qualis debeat esse in monasterio ubi abbas est, quicumque fuerit. But in P. L., vol. 67, col. 1099, this text is given as a single sentence, with a comma after Regula. In my previous translation, therefore, on p. 12 above, I took qualis as referring to Regula rather than to abbas. This seems the most natural interpretation, but does not agree with Cardinal Schuster's remark that St. Caesarius begins with the qualities of the abbot.

With St. Caesarius, minors had to make their renunciation verbally, to be confirmed with a legal act on the death of the parents (n. 1).

As to the boys, it seems instead that St. Benedict, after a sad experience, is correcting the arrangements of St. Caesarius in requiring that the parents themselves in the act of offering their son as a monk pledge themselves with an oath never to admit him to any part of their inheritance: "As regards their property . . . let everything be barred, so that the boy may have no expectations whereby he might be deceived and ruined, as we have learned by experience" (ch. 59).

But let us continue with the comparison:

"Let all things be common to you" (n. 2).

"Let all things be common to all" (ch. 33).

"They shall not swear" (n. 4).

"Not to swear, for fear of perjuring oneself. To utter truth from heart and mouth.

"Anyone who is caught lying shall receive the discipline of the law" (n. 5).

"They shall not curse" (n. 6).

"Not to curse those who curse us" (ch. 4).

"While they are at table eating, let no one speak, but let one of them read some book" (n. 9).

"The meals of the brethren should not be without reading. Nor should the reader be anyone who happens to take up the book" (ch. 38).

St. Benedict's precaution seems strange, that the table reader should not be just the first one to arrive, who would pick up a book and begin the reading, but that a weekly reader should rather be designated by the superior. Here the Patriarch of Cassino wants to clarify St. Caesarius' text, which he has before his eyes: "let one of them read some book". The sentence seemed ambiguous to him: the concern is certainly not with just any person and any book, but it is the superior who must determine the succession of readers and the choice of books.

"As long as we live in this body, let us fight day and night against the devil, with Christ as our helper and guide" (Rule for Monks, n. 26).

". . . while there is still time, while we are still in the body . . ." (prol.).

"They are able now, with no help save from God, to fight single-handed against the vices of the flesh and their own evil thoughts" (ch. 1).

"At every season let them read until Terce. After Terce let everyone do the work assigned him" (n. 14).

"Let them apply themselves to reading up to the end of the second hour . . . and then let all labor at the work assigned them until None" (ch. 48).

"Let no one receive anything secretly; especially let no one receive or deliver letters without the abbot's knowledge" (n. 15).

"On no account shall a monk be allowed to receive letters, tokens or any little gifts whatsoever from his parents or anyone else, or from his brethren, or to give the same, without the abbot's permission" (ch. 54).

"The abbot shall provide food and clothing . . . that

"Let clothing be given to the brethren . . . This is to be taken all may receive what things are necessary from the holy abbot" (n. 16).

into consideration, therefore, by the abbot" (ch. 55).

". . . But for all their necessities let them look to the father of the monastery" (ch. 33).

As is seen here, St. Benedict sometimes comes close to following the order of the canons of the Rule of St. Caesarius; for each number, a chapter of the Rule.

"Let the sick be treated in such a way that they will soon become well" (n. 17).

"On the Sick Brethren. Before all things and above all things, care must be taken of the sick . . ." (ch. 36).

At No. 19 in St. Caesarius there follows a sort of summary chapter which could be entitled "On the Good Zeal Which Monks Ought to Have":

"Have this contest among yourselves, who shall conquer the other through humility, through charity, who shall be less, who shall be more watchful in the Work of God, who shall have the greater patience, who shall be silent, meek, pleasant, penitent."

"For dinner and for supper only two dishes shall be

"This zeal, therefore, the monks should practice . . . Thus they should anticipate one another in honor; most patiently endure one another's infirmities, whether of body or of character; vie in paying obedience one to another — no one following what he considers useful for himself," etc. (ch. 72).

"For the daily dinner, whether at the sixth or the ninth hour prepared. Let them receive two drinks at dinner and at supper; and in time of fast, three . . ." (n. 22).

"Let the healthy never receive fowl and meat; let whatever is necessary be served to the sick" (n. 24).

. . . two cooked dishes . . . Therefore let two cooked dishes suffice for all the brethren . . .

"Except for the sick who are very weak, let all abstain entirely from eating the flesh of four-footed animals" (ch. 39).

"Let the weekly servers each receive a drink and some bread" (ch. 35).

From the comparison of these texts it appears evident how the Rule of St. Caesarius of Arles has served as a model for St. Benedict, who sometimes amends it instead of following it.

He had before his eyes also the Rule for nuns, in which Caesarius develops the canons of the preceding Rule and adapts them to female communities.

Here are some interesting comparisons:

ST. CAESARIUS

"While sitting at table let them be silent and pay attention to the reading . . . and let them ask for what is necessary by a nod rather than by speech" (n. 16).

"The sick are to be so treated that they may soon become well. But when they re-

ST. BENEDICT

"As to the things they need . . . If anything is needed, however, let it be asked for by means of some audible sign rather than by speech" (ch. 38).

"Let the use of meat be granted to the sick who are very weak, for the restoration of their

gain their former strength, they shall return to the happier custom of abstinence" (n. 20).

". . . that she secretly receives letters or any messages or little gifts from anyone", etc. (n. 23).

"The baths also which infirmity requires shall not be refused; but let it be done without murmuring, for medical reasons. . . . But if she is not compelled by any infirmity, her concupiscence shall not be encouraged" (n. 29).

"The care of the sick . . . should be assigned to one who is faithful and humble enough . . . and one should be chosen who . . . will serve the sick with piety" (n. 30).

"If any think that any clothes, shoes or utensils are to be used or kept carelessly, let them be severely corre t-ed, as embezzlers of the monastery's property" (n. 30).

"Whoever comes for the

strength; but when they are convalescent, let all abstain from meat as usual" (ch. 36).

"On no account shall a monk be allowed to receive letters, tokens or any little gifts whatsoever" (ch. 54).

"Let the use of baths be afforded the sick as often as may be expedient; but to the healthy, and especially to the young, let them be granted more rarely" (ch. 36).

". . . care of the sick . . . For these sick brethren let there be assigned a special room and an attendant who is God-fearing, diligent and solicitous" (ch. 36).

"If anyone treats the monastery's property in a slovenly or careless way, let him be corrected. If he fails to amend, let him undergo the discipline of the Rule" (ch. 32).

"When anyone is newly come

reformation of her life . . . let the Rule be read over to her frequently; and if she professes with a ready and free will that she will fulfil all the things set down in the Rule", etc. (Recapitulation, n. 8).

for the reformation of his life . . . let this Rule be read through to him . . . after the lapse of six months let the Rule be read to him . . . let the same Rule be read to him again. Then, having deliberated with himself, if he promises to keep it in its entirety and to observe everything that is commanded him", etc. (ch. 58).

To guarantee the integrity of the Rule after his death, St. Caesarius asked confirmation of it from Pope Hormisdas.[4] He himself alludes to this in the Recapitulation: "But study to fortify yourselves in all things with the help of the Lord, according to the sacred (precept) of the holy Father of Rome." It is hard to think that St. Benedict, who had before him the Rule of the metropolitan of Arles while drawing up his own, would have deprived himself of this guarantee.

* * *

But the comparisons which I have just made here between the two codes tell us another thing also. They demonstrate that the twofold regulation of St. Caesarius, for monks and for nuns, served as a fabric for St. Benedict on which to embroider the Rule for Monks. Some details seem to acquire a new light and a clearer meaning when they are compared with the corresponding Caesarian text. Even the terminology adopted by St. Benedict — "the Work of God . . . to come for the reformation of one's life . . . a drink . . . a token . . . let him receive the discipline . . . in the presence of the community . . . the Holy Rule", etc. — is derived from the bishop of Arles.

Caesarius, imitated by the Patriarch of Cassino, is certainly calling his work a "Holy Rule" when he expressly declares that it has been "written according to the instruction of the holy Fathers". Here we have an explanation, therefore, of the meaning which St. Benedict also gives to this expression "Holy Rule".

* * *

But how and when did the abbot of Subiaco or of Monte Cassino become acquainted with the Caesarian monastic codes? This is impossible to determine; but it is certain that before the Rules of St. Caesarius made their triumphal circuit in the monasteries of Gaul, Germany and even Italy, the author himself had gone to Rome in 513.

From the time of Pope Symmachus up to the year of his death in 543, Caesarius had been in continual correspondence with no less than seven Pontiffs, with whose approval he had been accustomed to regulate his whole metropolitan activity. His stay in Rome lasted several months, from autumn of 513 to Easter of 514. During these very years St. Benedict was developing his monastic institute among the Simbruini mountains as well as on Monte Cassino. Thus it is not very surprising that the Patriarch of Cassino was stitching his own embroidery on the fabric of the Caesarian Rules, for the precise purpose of bringing Italian monachism to that unity of observance and of spirit at which the French metropolitan was likewise aiming.

In the bishop of Arles, however, such initiative entered perfectly into the competence of his legislative mission as metropolitan and vicar of the Holy See. But as for St. Benedict, who follows in his footsteps, not being either a bishop or a representative of the Pope, by whose commission does he write?

His own personal initiative appears most unlikely; we must conclude that the example of St. Caesarius, already praised and approved by Pope Hormisdas, had finally decided the Apostolic See to introduce into Italy also through the work of the Cassinese Wonder-Worker that monastic unification which, under the auspices of Caesarius, was promising so much good in Gaul.

* * *

The better to understand such a commission, it is opportune to keep in mind the sad conditions in which the Apostolic See had come to find itself during almost the entire life of St. Benedict. During the schism of the antipope Lawrence, Ennodius of Pavia under his own guarantee had money lent to Pope Symmachus from the bishop of Milan! Symmachus then had given carte blanche to Ennodius to act in his name in this affair of the schism.

"I have a letter from the Pope", wrote Ennodius to Luminosus, "in which he ordered that whatever had to be done should be completed with my security."[5]

Another contemporary of St. Benedict at Rome was the monk Dionysius Exiguus (died about 540), who, by commission of Pope Hormisdas (514-523), gathered the Greek synodal canons into one Greek-Latin collection, unfortunately lost.

* * *

A propos of the Rule for Monks deposited about 586 in the papal archives as a measure of security, we know that in St. Benedict's last years, about 544, there had been received into those archives as a most important document also the poem On the Acts of the Apostles by the subdeacon Arator. The prefect of the pontifical scrinium at that time was one Surgentius. The educated people of Rome were not content, however, with that honorable custody, but wanted the author to recite the most beautiful parts of his poem in the church itself. The recitation followed in the basilica of St. Peter in Chains on four different days of April and May, 544, to the lively satisfaction of Pope Vigilius and the Romans.

* * *

It is known that one of the sources on which St. Benedict drew largely in the Rule was Cassian with his Conferences and Monastic Institutes.

The origin of this vast work conceived as divided in two parts is as follows.

Bishop Castor of Apta Iulia in Narbonese Gaul, having founded a monastery near his episcopal city, wanted to profit from Cassian's knowledge of the Rules and the way of life followed by the monks of Egypt and Palestine.

To please the prelate, in about the year 420 Cassian composed his work, which, almost immediately translated into Greek also, very quickly became a sort of foundation for the whole monastic discipline of the West in the early Middle Ages.

But there is a difference between the Rule of St. Benedict and the work of Cassian. The latter is simply a manual of ascetical life; to give it the force of law, the episcopal authority must intervene to impose it. The Rule for Monks, on the other hand, already takes the form of general laws, and gives the impression that a universal ecclesiastical authority has intervened in its very drafting to approve of that form.

* * *

In 440 St. Leo I succeeded Pope Sixtus II. He was in Gaul at the time of his election. On his departure for Rome he brought with him Prosper of Aquitaine, to whom he then assigned an office in the pontifical chancellery.

We are informed by Gennadius that "the letters also of Pope Leo against Eutyches on the true incarnation of Christ, addressed to various persons, are supposed to have been dictated by him (Prosper)" (Gennadius, De Viris Illustribus, 84-85).

St. Benedict's Personality in the "Rule"

Now, notwithstanding the thousand juridical reasons which exclude the possibility that a simple abbot of Monte Cassino — who had become in addition a missionary in a zone of the Campania Felix still dominated by paganism — would have had authority to prescribe a single Rule for the whole of Italian monachism, St. Benedict did just that.

The Rule for Monks, rather than being an abstract law which is addressed, like a manual of ascetics, to hypothetical disciples, represents the powerful personality of a definite, well known teacher and lawgiver who is teaching his subjects or pupils.

Even if it were not explicitly stated, the definition of the Benedictine monastery as "a school for the service of the Lord" could be seen in the spirit of the Rule. But this spiritual teaching itself is presented to us as a work essentially personal: it is St. Benedict and no one else who is teaching and prescribing.

There are few spiritual books in which the author's personality dominates the teaching as strongly as it does in the Rule for Monks. From the first page to the last, the writer openly takes the responsibility for what he is teaching: he wants to appear always as a teacher, and for him the readers are simply disciples, nothing more.

As these disciples are to be found not only in the limited circle of the Cassinese citadel, St. Benedict in the Rule already assumes that majestic attitude of Patriarch of Western monachism which in fact the later history of the whole Middle Ages acknowledged as his right.

If we were to suppose that the characteristic notes of this powerful personality which shines through the Rule were merely the result of some editorial retouching when Abbot Simplicius published the text outside of Monte Cassino, we still would not have solved the problem of the Rule's authority. For there was certainly nothing in the time or the conditions of Abbot Simplicius that could project the colossal figure of St. Benedict on the future history of Europe.

Moreover, nothing authorizes us to suppose that Simplicius may have interpolated the Rule in order to glorify the Master. Instead, he was jealously guarding the autograph manuscript of it. Then as for unduly exalting St. Benedict, at Monte Cassino he was so little esteemed that the merits and glory of Simplicius himself were equated with those of St. Benedict: the one because he had written the Rule, the other because he had published it:

"He published the Master's hidden work for all.

Yet one reward remains to both forever."

The powerful personality of St. Benedict shown in the Rule is therefore his authentic work.

Let us gather some texts in which this personality is most strongly affirmed, as proof against contrary theses:

"Listen, my son, to your master's precepts . . . your loving father's advice . . . To you, therefore, my words are now addressed . . .

"And so we are going to establish a school for the service of the Lord. In founding it we hope to introduce nothing harsh or burdensome" (prol.).

"Let us proceed . . . to lay down a rule for the strongest kind of monks, the cenobites" (ch. 1).

"But as for coarse jests . . . th se we condemn everywhere with a perpetual ban, and for such conversation we do not permit a disciple to open his mouth" (ch. 6).

"For we call our body and soul the sides of the ladder" (ch. 7).

"We strongly recommend, however, that if this distribution of the psalms is displeasing to anyone, he should arrange them otherwise, in whatever way he considers better" (ch. 18).

"And we order the same to be done in the case of the prior" (ch. 21).

"It is therefore with some misgivings that we regulate the measure of other men's sustenance" (ch. 40).

"The reason why we have judged it fitting for them to stand in the last place . . ." (ch. 43).

"To that end we think that the times for each may be prescribed as follows" (ch. 48).

"We believe, however, that in ordinary places the following dress is sufficient for each monk: a tunic, a cowl . . ." (ch. 55).

". . . so that the boy may have no expectations whereby (which God forbid) he might be deceived and ruined, as we have learned by experience" (ch. 59).

"By this we do not mean that he should allow vices to grow; on the contrary, as we have already said, he should eradicate them prudently and with charity" (ch. 64).

"To us, therefore, it seems expedient for the preservation of peace and charity that the abbot have in his hands the full administration of his monastery" (ch. 65).

"We desire that this Rule be read often in the community" (ch. 66).

"Now we have written this Rule in order that by its observance in monasteries . . .

". . . fulfil with the help of Christ this minimum Rule which we have written for beginners" (ch. 73).

Analyzing more carefully these solemn affirmations of the personality of the Rule's author, we notice in them two different attitudes of mind: the humility of the Saint, which is readily seen in the words "for us who are lazy and ill-living and negligent they are a source of shame and confusion"; and the majesty of the Lawgiver and Master, who says without hesitation, "Let us proceed, with God's help, to lay down a rule for the strongest kind of monks, the cenobites."

The actual text of the Rule, as I have said, with its chapters duplicated or redundant, seems to let two different drafts show through, which, instead of being fused into one definitive edition, were sewn together just as the author had laid them out. The study of the sources has already been made in part, and to pursue it here would carry me too far afield.

Possibly, too, one or another chapter of the Rule still preserves large quotations from sermons for certain occasions, preached by St. Benedict before his Cassinese community.

Thus, for example, in the chapter "On the Observance of Lent"

(49), the orator, besides getting his inspiration from the Lenten sermons of St. Leo the Great, repeatedly indicates the coincidence of the Lenten season in which he also is preaching.

"We therefore urge that during these days of Lent . . . wash away during these holy days . . .

"During these days, therefore, let us increase somewhat . . .

In chapter 7 also, "On Humility", except for the quotations from Cassian the style is obviously oratorical, and the preacher repeatedly apostrophizes those present, calling them "brethren".

"Holy Scripture, brethren, cries out to us, saying . . . Hence, brethren, if we wish to reach the very highest point of humility . . ."

There follows the exegesis of the Scriptural ladder of Jacob with the orator's personal interpretation:

"By that descent and ascent we must surely understand nothing else than this . . ." This exegetical interpretation, expressed with so much authority, resembles Augustine or Jerome or some Pontiff preaching.

"For we call our body and soul the sides of the ladder . . .

"We must constantly beware, brethren, as the Prophet says in the psalm . . ."

This homiletic exegesis contained in the Rule is precisely in the style of the various Treatises or patristic sermons of the epoch.

* * *

In rereading the Rule we can notice at once that several chapters have moreover a striking analogy with the style of the pontifical constitutions and letters of the time. In both kinds of documents first a canonical principle or scriptural maxim is affirmed or quoted; then the practical application is derived from it: "Therefore . . .;

hence . . .; for that reason . . ."

Here are some examples:

RULE OF ST. BENEDICT

"The first degree of humility is obedience without delay. This is the virtue of those who . . ." (ch. 5).

"Let us do what the Prophet says: 'I said, "I will guard my ways, that I may not sin . . ." ' Therefore, since the spirit of silence . . ." (ch. 6).

"Holy Scripture, brethren, cries out to us, saying . . . When it says this, therefore, it shows us . . . Hence, brethren . . ." (ch. 7).

"The measure of excommunication or of chastisement should correspond to the degree of fault, which degree is estimated by the abbot's judgment" (ch. 24).

"Every age and degree of understanding should have its proper measure of discipline. Therefore . . ." (ch. 30).

"Although human nature itself is drawn to special kindness . . . towards old men and children, still the authority of the Rule should also provide for them" (ch. 37).

"The meals of the brethren should not be without reading . . . there should be a reader for the whole week, entering that office on Sunday" (ch. 38).

" 'Everyone has his own gift from God, one in this way and another in that.' It is therefore . . ." (ch. 40).

"Monks ought to be zealous for silence at all times . . . And therefore . . ." (ch. 42).

"Idleness is the enemy of the soul. Therefore . . ." (ch. 48).

". . . The life of a monk ought to have about it at all times the character of a Lenten observance . . . we therefore urge . . ." (ch. 49).

"Let the oratory be what it is called, a place of prayer; and let nothing else . . ." (ch. 52).

Many of the letters of St. Gregory I are written on the same plan: first a general principle, then the application to the particular case by means of a conjunction of agreement, as "therefore", "because", etc.

Here are some examples, among many.

"Whenever any matter is entrusted to several persons to be done, when one dissents from the other the way is left open to expense rather than to profit. Foreseeing this, we" etc. (book 1, n. 81).

"A church set up in a fortified place should not be without the attention of a pastor. Because therefore . . . for that reason" etc. (book 2, n. 16).

"Just as a person is rightly barred from the sacrament of Communion when guilt requires, so such punishment should in no way be inflicted on the innocent . . . and for that reason" etc. (book 3, n. 26).

"Religious desires should be put into execution without difficulty. And for that reason" etc. (book 3, n. 63).

"It is neither proper nor expedient for us to pass by those things which pertain to the correction of religious persons . . . . And for that reason" etc. (book 5, n. 50).

* * *

The problem indicated above, as to how St. Benedict, without being either Pope or bishop, could have written the Rule for Monks "to lay down a rule for the strongest kind of monks, the cenobites" (Rule, ch. 1), is now posed, but not yet solved.

That is to say, the psychology of the writer is not explained, setting himself up on a pedestal which only the later centuries have erected for him. Nor is it explained, either, how the contemporary world, without objection or debate, almost at once after the death of St. Benedict, recognized his code as the unique Rule for Monks and quickly adopted it.

Evidently, the contemporary world must have felt itself confronted with an extraordinary, powerful personality, on which heaven with prodigies, earth with prestige and the ecclesiastical hierarchy with quite ample favor were conferring an extraordinary authority which the mere abbot of Monte Cassino would never have been able to assume by himself.

Gaps in the Gregorian Biography of St. Benedict

St. Gregory's story of St. Benedict is no more than a mere floretum of miracles. His true and proper history Gregory unfortunately did not write, nor did he know it in its entirety, because it did not enter into the plan of his Dialogs: "I have not been able to learn all that he did" (prol.). The poet Mark in his poem on St. Benedict adds some valuable details quite independent of St. Gregory's biography; but unfortunately they are few, too late and mixed with a poor kind of poetry.

The same St. Gregory later, in book 3, chapter 16, of the Dialogs, comes back incidentally to speak of St. Benedict, and relates to us a new, untold episode, pervaded with seraphic charm.

How deplorable it is, then, that none of his contemporaries left us a biography of St. Benedict, and that we therefore find ourselves unable at this late date to reconstruct it entirely!

If we had the good fortune to possess such a History, or at least a Regestum Casinense, we would perhaps find documented there the relations of the Patriarch with the civil authorities, with the Popes of his time, with the bishops of the region of Campania, with Cassiodorus, with Theodoric, with Totila and his first ministers, etc.

These documents would give us a better understanding of several points: for example, with what authority St. Benedict, about 530, left the government of the first twelve monasteries at Subiaco and went to Cassino to dedicate himself to the new mission of converting infidels; by whom and how he was given the fortress with the annexed temples, which at that time were government property; how the monastery came into possession of that villa of which St. Gregory speaks in the Dialogs, book 2, chapter 33: "On these occasions he would go down to meet her in a house belonging to the monastery a short distance from the entrance." There were also other property-holders, therefore, on the Cassinese mountain!

St. Benedict and the Ecclesiastical Jurisdiction

Also to be clarified are the ecclesiastical relations between St. Benedict and those "villages" which had been converted to the faith by him.

Into one of those villages, where some consecrated virgins lived, he used to dispatch one of his monks rather often "to exhort souls", to give sermons. We see that the Saint exercised such ecclesiastical authority over these religious women that his twofold sentence on the sharp-tongued virgins, first of excommunication and then of absolution, was ratified even in heaven. It is to be noticed, moreover, that in this "village" there was already a church with clergy attached, charged with the sacred functions. Yet it is St. Benedict at Monte Cassino who admonishes and threatens the nuns, and after their death it is he who absolves them: "Have this

41

offered up for their souls during the holy Sacrifice, and they will be freed from the sentence of excommunication" (ch. 23). Pope Zachary in his Greek version of the Dialogs makes it clear that this is a true and proper sentence of excommunication and of absolution.

The difficulty which the interlocutor, the deacon Peter, poses to St. Gregory on this subject does not even touch — and this is important — on St. Benedict's authority to threaten or inflict excommunication, but rather on the circumstance of his having absolved souls when they had already departed this life: "Is it not extraordinary that souls already judged at God's invisible tribunal could be pardoned by him?" The Pontiff replies that divine authority was granted St. Peter to loose and to bind on earth and in heaven. "All those who govern the Church in matters of faith and morals exercise the same power of binding and loosing that he received."

The concern, therefore, is with a true priestly condemnation and absolution, which has this special note about it, its efficacy "by the faith and morals" of the Saint even when the souls of the deceased were already beyond the competence of the shepherds of the Church militant!

* * *

The other deed narrated by St. Gregory in chapter 24 has some affinity with this post mortem absolution. The concern was with a young monk who had fled from the Cassinese monastery and whose body for that reason the earth kept rejecting. His parents went up desperately to Monte Cassino and with great cries and tears, as is still the manner with people of that kind, begged Benedict "to restore the boy to his favor". There is question of another excommunication, therefore, and this one involved also the fugitive's body which not even the earth would welcome to her maternal bosom: "since not even the earth would retain the young monk's body until he had been reconciled with blessed Benedict."

What does the Saint do then? As a sign of absolution and of re-admission to ecclesiastical communion, "the man of God at once gave them with his own hand the Communion[6] of the Body of the Lord and said, 'Go and lay the Body of the Lord upon his breast with great reverence and bury him once more.' " The absolution from the excommunication comes from the Eucharistic Communion, which the Saint "with his own hand" sends to the dead one by means of his afflicted parents. In the Greek version of Pope St. Zachary it is said more clearly: Benedict breaks off "a particle of the Body of the Lord" and hands it to the parents. Λαβὼν ἀπὸ τοῦ δεσποτικοῦ σώματος μερίδα μίαν δέδωκεν.

The rite is well known to liturgists, and at one time was also quite common in the whole Church. The bishops and the priests in some circumstances used to send the parishes subject to them a detached particle of the "Eucharist itself",[7] as a sign of ecclesiastical communion. Enclosed in precious wrappings, it was also placed on the breast of the deceased, as a pledge of communion with the Church and an earnest of resurrection.

In the particular case described by St. Gregory, the sacred fragment detached from the Saint's Eucharist — and therefore at the appointed time during the Mass — and consigned "with his own hand" to the dead one's parents, was simply a sign that the deceased was absolved from the excommunication and restored to the favor of his spiritual father.

It is St. Benedict, therefore, who "at once gave them with his own hand the Communion of the Body of the Lord". In saying this St. Gregory describes the Patriarch of monachism in the act of

43

celebrating the divine Sacrifice and of performing the "breaking" of the sacred Mysteries. Being no longer able to restore the living person to Communion, "with his own hand" he grants the Eucharist and has it put upon the dead person to absolve him from the excommunication.

St. Gregory's whole account establishes quite clearly that in this second case of the runaway monk, as in the case of the talkative nuns, St. Benedict's action was not a mere practice of Eucharistic devotion but a real absolution and consequent readmission of the culprit to the sacred Communion; and this, if you please, not of a living person but of a deceased one!

In chapter 23 as well as in chapter 24, therefore, St. Gregory depicts St. Benedict in the exercise of his priestly function of the "Breaking of the Bread" in favor of a deceased person; of loosing and of binding souls on earth as in the world beyond; of refusing and of granting "with his own hand" to his own subjects, monks and consecrated virgins, Communion in the Body of the Lord; of occupying, in a word, "the place of the holy See by faith and morals", as St. Gregory says.

This priestly ministry helps us to understand his legislative authority in the monastic domain, and at the same time also the fruitfulness of the holy Patriarch's missionary apostolate among the Cassinese idolaters: "Gradually the people of the countryside were won over to the true faith by his zealous preaching" (ch. 8).[8]

Missionary Activity in the Region of Casinum

Such an apostolate in the midst of the pagans must have been neither easy nor brief, when it is considered that the Cassinese acropolis, on the word of the poet Mark, was a kind of pantheon where the last relics of idolatry had sought asylum in a wild death-agony. And yet even large villages were won to the Catholic faith, for instance the one of which St. Gregory writes: "Not far from the monastery was a village in which lived not a few persons converted from the worship of idols to the true faith by Benedict's instructions" (ch. 19).

This brings us back to the juridical question: How could St. Benedict assume for himself possession of property belonging to the state, of a "sacred place", to change its use? Aside from the resistance which those infuriated idolaters must have offered him, how could he of his own initiative and choice convert idolatrous temples into Christian churches? Here we are helped directly by a law of the Theodosian code (book 16, title X-20, year 415): "The Christian religion rightly claims for itself those places assigned to sacred things by the error of those who went before . . . which by manifold agreements shall belong, as we have decided, to the venerable Church."

At the very time when St. Benedict migrated from Subiaco to Monte Cassino, the Emperor Justinian was attending to the inclusion of those laws of Theodosius in the new "Body of Civil Law". St. Benedict's work on Monte Cassino, therefore, was perfectly lawful. But such a claim on the ancient pagan sanctuaries could be made not be mere private persons but by the "venerable Church". For that reason, in the margin of the Gregorian narration of how St. Benedict reassigned the government of the monasteries of Subiaco and went to convert the region of Casinum, we must see likewise the story of all the long and laborious negotiations between the ecclesiastical and the civil authority which would have to precede the transfer of those old temples to the Catholic Church. The cession, according to law, had to be done not to a private person but to the "Christian religion"; and if St. Benedict took them over, he must undoubtedly have acted in the name of the Pope or of the bishop of the diocese. This juridical condition of the Cassinese mission throws a new light on the evangelizing work of the Patriarch of monks and on his personal relations with the highest authorities of his time.

In view of the desperate resistance of the pagans of the territory of Aquino to becoming converted to the faith and to ceding to the "Christian religion" their old temples on the summit of Monte Cassino, it is quite probable that the authority of the apostolic See itself, in claiming those "sacred places" from the domain of the state, destined for that difficult mission none other than St. Benedict, whose fame by that time had filled Rome also.

The obscene persecution on the part of the priest Florentius at Subiaco was therefore simply the external occasion that determined St. Benedict to undertake that arduous enterprise.

So true is this that, when the tragic death of his persecutor was suddenly announced to the Saint, he would not comply with the invitation of Maurus to turn back; but instead he pursued his way boldly, in wholly supernatural conditions and atmosphere, as the poet-monk Mark reports. St. Benedict, therefore, considered his mission at Subiaco as closed: his life was now about to enter a new phase. After the anchoretic and monastic life among the Simbruini mountains there now follows the priestly apostolate among the pagans and the codification of a Rule for Monks, which the Holy See in its own time can impose universally.

With his transfer to Monte Cassino St. Benedict is imprinting on Western monachism an entirely new spirit, exactly the kind of spirit required by the new world the Church is about to reconstruct.

* * *

The authority and the importance which clothe the figure of St. Benedict in the contemporary world reflect another light also on the Rule for Monks. The one who is drawing up those laws is an apostle powerful in works and eloquence, to whom the bishop or the Pope has entrusted an important and difficult missionary enterprise.

On St. Benedict's going to Casinum, "when the man of God arrived at this spot, he destroyed the idol, overturned the altar and cut down the trees in the sacred groves. Then he turned the temple of Apollo into a chapel dedicated to St. Martin; and where Apollo's altar had stood, he built a chapel in honor of St. John the Baptist. Gradually the people of the countryside were won over to the true faith by his zealous preaching."

Reading over these lines of St. Gregory, the mind readily goes back to the similar deeds of Eliseus and of St. John the Baptist, yet not forgetting that all this vigorous evangelical campaign must have required long years of hard labor (530?-547?).

And the pagans? The biographer does not even mention them; but he records instead that the devil himself appeared to St. Benedict and threatened him, with eyes and lips spewing fire. If the devil did thus, his sons certainly would not have done less than their father!

The poet Mark indicates another episode omitted by St. Gregory: the people of the Cassinese territory, recently won over to the faith, besiege St. Benedict, shut up in his Roman tower, awaiting in retirement and penance the hour to go out and begin the sacred Vigils of the night of the Resurrection.

"Here too the people, on your word, lay siege to your retreat,
While you await the sacred night's solemnities."

This liturgical detail also has its importance. We know that, especially in the East, the more devout used to pass holy Lent in strict retirement and solitude, and return to the customs of ordinary life on the solemnity of Easter. At Alexandria, for example, the patriarch would retire to observe the Lenten fast among the monks in the desert, where on Maundy Thursday he would even consecrate the holy oils, and would reappear in the city among his faithful in the night of the holy Paschal Vigil.

St. Benedict does the same at Monte Cassino. But the devotion of those people is such that, though the country sky is not yet sparkling with stars in the silver splendor of the vernal full moon, they, the newly converted, are already at the foot of the Cassinese tower, waiting for St. Benedict to come out and begin the sacred Vigils of Easter: "While you await the sacred night's solemnities."

But have not these neophytes their priests in their own "villages", who can perform the functions of the Paschal night, just as the good curate of Monte Porcaro used to do, according to St. Gregory's story? And yet the people are already at Monte Cassino hours before the functions, calling for St. Benedict to come out of the tower, that the sacred rites may begin.

This liturgical detail also has its importance for our knowledge of St. Benedict.

Relations with the Powerful

Around 542, when King Totila invaded the Campania and Samnium, having heard of the fame of the Cassinese Wonder-Worker regarded as a new prophet, he showed a desire to make his acquaintance personally.

He did not treat him, however, as just some undistinguished hermit. Having become accustomed to the Roman rules of protocol, the king first gave orders to have himself announced to the "great man", and he meanwhile waited in a nearby place.

From the monastery comes the dignified response that he should come: "He received answer from the monastery that he might come." The reply gives the same impression, that at Monte Cassino dwells a sovereign who deigns to grant audience to a foreign monarch!

Totila, however, superstitious and barbarous, devises the masquerade of his three courtiers, whom he sends to Monte Cassino to simulate the royal visit and thereby test the Saint's prophetic spirit. When the game is discovered the king decides to go up to the mountain and see the prophet. But when he can barely see Benedict from a distance, he falls to his knees in terror. Notwithstanding the Saint's invitation to rise and come forward, Totila does not dare get up until St. Benedict himself comes to help him up and bring him into the monastery.

The conversation which followed between Totila and the Abbot was very dramatic. A Cassinese chronicler of the eleventh century was even able to point out the precise place where Benedict carrivit ad Totila, so faithfully had tradition preserved this point of knowledge as a most memorable fact! St. Gregory's account tells us that the Wonder-Worker knew so well how to interweave reprimands, threats and hopes of future triumphs that, before leaving, the king wanted his priestly blessing, which was then granted by reciting the liturgical collect: "Terrified at these words, the king asked for a blessing and went away" (Dialogs, book 2, ch. 15).

"Orationem Dare"

The Gregorian expression orationem petiit was at that time proper to the liturgical language, and referred to the blessing or collect which bishops and priests used to invoke upon the faithful, especially at the end of the sacred service.

Still to this day in the Roman Missal, during Lent, the deacon bids the people Humiliate capita vestra Deo before the priest recites the final collect of blessing over them after the Communion. To this Roman rite corresponds the formula of the Milanese deacon, who, before the prayer of blessing of his archbishop, still today cries to the people, Humiliate vos ad benedictionem.

On November 22, 545, when Pope Vigilius was snatched away from the altar of the basilica of St. Cecilia across the Tiber, and was dragged to the ship awaiting below on the river to take him to Byzantium, the Roman people made tumultuous complaint because time was not granted the Pontiff to pronounce the final prayer of blessing. The Greek guard, terrified by the fury of the people, who were torn into factions, had to give in. Vigilius, standing upright in the boat, was thus able to recite over the Romans the collect of blessing. The one party answered "Amen", while the Pope's adversaries concluded the prayer with another litany of imprecations.

St. Gregory also refers to this liturgical rite of blessing in chapter 13 of book 2 of the Dialogs. The brother of the future Abbot Valentinian made a pilgrimage every year to Monte Cassino "that he might receive the prayer of the Servant of God", and at the same time also to see his brother. With that intention, and in order that the Saint's blessing might find him better disposed, he used to go there fasting. One of these times, however, after a little lunch along the way, he arrives at Monte Cassino at dusk. He is soon presented to St. Benedict, of whom "he asked for the blessing" (sibi orationem dari petiit). The phrase is equivalent to the one above: the guest asks that the "collect of blessing" be recited over him. But thereupon St. Benedict reveals to him the temptation to which he had yielded shortly before, and reproves him for the offense of imploring that blessing, kneeling at his feet, to be sure,

50

but without having fasted also! "He fell at Benedict's feet and admitted the weakness of his will." Pope Zachary translates in the Greek: "Prostrate on the ground, he asked to receive the prayer of blessing . . . εὐχὴν ἠτησατο λαβεῖν."

St. Benedict in the Opinion of His Contemporaries

From the very beginning of his biography of St. Benedict, Gregory declares that he does not by any means know all the Patriarch's works, but only some of the most impressive episodes: "I was unable to learn about all his miraculous deeds, but the few that I am going to relate . . . " (book 2, prol.).

Nevertheless it is interesting that the historian, so restricted in sources of information, makes his hero live in close relations not only with his monks but with the whole outside contemporary world.

There are the bishops of Aquino, Capua and Canosa who maintain friendly relations with him. The abbot and deacon Servandus is often his welcome guest at Monte Cassino. A landowner of Terracina engages him to found a monastery in that city. Members of the clergy, poor peasants, debtors hard pressed, poor victims of the brutality of the Goths, needy people of every sort — all have recourse in their needs to Monte Cassino and come for aid from the charity of the common Father of souls.

The poor of the countryside even go so far as to demand of him the resurrection of their dead. To such a pretentious thing the Saint protests futilely, observing that they wanted to put on his back a load too heavy for his shoulders, such as only the holy Apostles in Rome could carry. "Stand back, brethren! Stand back! Such a miracle is beyond our power. The holy Apostles are the only ones who can raise the dead. Why would you place a burden upon us that we cannot bear?" (ch. 32). In speaking or in writing, St. Benedict employs only the "we" of majesty!

But what happened? The insistence of the poor father, grief-stricken before the rigid little body of his son, which he had put on the threshold of the Cassinese monastery, finally prevailed over the humility of the Wonder-Worker, who in the end had to yield and revive the dead one.

The thing we should notice in this prodigy, however, is the popular opinion which attributed to St. Benedict such power over life and death.

* * *

There is another interesting sketch drawn by St. Gregory in chapter 20 of the Life. It is now evening, and St. Benedict on that day must have returned late to the monastery. For he is taking his food outside of the prescribed hour, and therefore without the usual table companions of the abbot, who, as the Rule prescribes, are always the guests and the pilgrims.

Near the table a young monk stands holding the light, while in the nearby kitchen other monks are lending their services. Most of the community meanwhile have gone to their night's rest.

All at once St. Benedict cries to the young monk holding the light, "What are you murmuring about in your heart? Sign your heart with the Cross!" And calling the monks from the kitchen, he has the lamp-bearer give the light to another and go to bed without further ado.

The young monk passes the candlestick to another, but his colleagues, wide-eyed, ask him whatever may have happened to him. And he, already halfway exposed, had to confess that, his father being a _defensor_[9] of the Church, he had nourished in his heart a certain feeling of pride and resentment at having been chosen for such a service proper to a slave. The Abbot had read his heart.

"Who is this", the vain monk had been thinking, "that I should have to stand here holding the lamp for him while he is eating? Who am I to be serving him?"

Here again we find ourselves in the presence of a singular personality, who even in externals guards the prestige and the respect due to his rank. For this it was not enough to put the candlestick on the table! No; Roman patrician custom, which had passed also into the ecclesiastical world, required that servants and lower clerics be appointed to hold it before the _dominus_ or the priest. St. Benedict at Monte Cassino had not rejected this rule of etiquette.

Evidently, between the anchorite of Subiaco, who goes out to get the food when Romanus lowers it to him by a rope down the mountain with the sound of a bell, and St. Benedict, who dines at Monte Cassino with the son of a _defensor_ having to stand by the table and hold the candlestick, there must intervene some great fact which has somewhat modified the outward conduct of the Wonder-Worker. Is not this external fact perhaps the evangelizing mission, or is it the priestly rank conferred on him by the highest authority of the Church? Without that explanation the psychological problem is hard to solve.

Now there arises the question: Under what bishop did St. Benedict live? Who had consecrated his churches at Subiaco and in the Cassinese territory? Who had authorized his mission among the pagans? Who had given the chrism to his neophytes? Who had put him in possession of the Cassinese fortress and temples?

53

The Origins of the "Ius Regularium"

From the pontifical correspondence, especially the letters of St. Gregory the Great, we can see that Italy at that time was all dotted with little dioceses and with monasteries. The pontifical and episcopal rights were now well established, developed and extended, down to the least circumstance of the monastic and clerical life; so that very little was left to the free initiative of individuals.

Here are some examples:

Abbot Sabinus of St. Stephanus of Capri has some relics of St. Agatha with which he wants to have his church consecrated. He must turn to the Pope, however. The Pope then gives orders to the bishop of Sorrentum to proceed to that consecration (Letters, book 1, n. 54).

From the numerous letters of Gregory to the bishops, granting them permission to consecrate churches and private oratories, it seems established that at that time such a right was reserved to the Roman Pontiff, at least in the circuit of his metropolitan province, which hardly excluded Ravenna and Milan.[10]

Venantius, bishop of Luni, had asked authorization to consecrate the monastery of virgins he had founded in the house where he was born. The Pope grants it to him; but in such a circumstance he inserts into the rescript the inventory of the patrimony assigned to the new foundation. The oratory with the altar, therefore, will contain the relics of SS. Peter, John and Paul, Irma and Sebastian; first, however, it will have to be agreed that in the chapel there be no other tombs near the sacred altar. The founder, moreover, will have to make legal donation of the new monastery's dowry: "that is: one silver chalice weighing six ounces, a silver paten weighing two pounds, two syndones, one altar covering, ten beds made up, twenty heads in bronze, thirty heads in iron, in land the Fabaorian estate and Lubricata constituted wholly in the territory of Luni, between one and two miles from the city, by the river Magra, with two slaves, that is, Maurus and John, and only two pairs of oxen. The municipal deeds being bound, you will consecrate the oratory of the aforesaid monastery solemnly, without public Mass" (book 8, n. 4).

In the rescript the expressions "you desire the monastery to be consecrated" and "you will consecrate the oratory" are equivalent, just as they are when St. Gregory speaks of the twelve monasteries or oratories at Subiaco: "He reorganized all the monasteries (oratoria) he had founded, appointing priors to assist in governing them."

Considering the law of the time, it is impossible to think of the erection of those twelve chapels at Subiaco without the consent and intervention of the bishop who had to consecrate them, and without the probable permission of the Roman Pontiff as metropolitan of the place (Dialogs, book 2, ch. 8).

The inventory of the monastery inserted in the pontifical document to the bishop of Luni might give us an idea of that other document to which St. Benedict refers a propos of the cellarer: "The abbot shall keep a list of these articles, so that as the brethren succeed one another in their assignments he may know what he gives and what he receives back" (ch. 32, "On the Tools and Property of the Monastery").

* * *

In the juridical spirit of the time, the important fact which determined the Pope or the bishop to the inauguration of a monastery with the consecration of the annexed oratory was the depositing of the relics of the martyrs who were to be venerated there. The monastery and the chapel would take the name of the same saints whose relics were preserved under the altar table.

Hence when St. Benedict has the new monk make his religious profession "in the name of the saints whose relics are there" (ch. 58), he is referring precisely to this canonical discipline.

Being habituated to our recent customs and to the numerous privileges of the regulars, we too often reconstruct ancient history with materials of modern make. Today, erecting an inside chapel for Sisters or Brothers is a thing which can be quickly done by their own local superior. There need only be inserted in the constructed altar a sacred stone already consecrated, and the chapel is in order

It was not at all so in the ancient discipline, especially in the sixth and seventh centuries. In order to erect altars, chapels, baptistries, very often the bishop's authority was not even sufficient in the Pope's metropolitan district it was necessary also to apply to the Pontiff in Rome for the desired relics of a martyr. The Pope would then order the bishop in whose diocese the martyr's tomb was located to grant the favor requested. Such relics generally consisted simply of veils which had covered, or at least had been brought near, the saint's tomb.

When the relics had been obtained, they were transmitted to the local bishop of the new monastery to be dedicated. Finally when everything was in order and the canonical conditions required by the prevailing law were fully satisfied, the bishop would proceed to the solemn consecration of the new oratory. The admission of the public at large to his Mass was avoided, however, that the laws of enclosure might be perfectly observed. A great number of ecclesiastics would come to the Mass, and the poor would receive extraordinary and abundant help.

St. Benedict also must undoubtedly have obeyed this discipline for the twelve oratories at Subiaco as well as for the various churches which he erected both in the Cassinese monastery and in the villages converted by him to the Christian faith.

An example serves to illustrate this whole canonico-liturgical procedure. A "religious woman, Januaria", had asked St. Gregory to grant her permission to have an oratory of hers consecrated in honor of St. Severinus, confessor, and St. Juliana, martyr. As the bodies of the two saints were kept in the diocese of Naples, the Pope wrote to Bishop Fortunatus of Naples that he should promptly grant the desired relics (Letters, book 9, n. 85). The style of the pontifical chancery does not allow for compliments. As the new oratory could not be dedicated to the two saints without the given relics, "that in their name the oratory . . . may be solemnly con-secrated . . . and therefore, dear brother, it behooves you to obey the desires of the above-mentioned woman, by reason of our com-mand, that she may obtain the result of her devotion in the conse-cration for which she is asking." Gregory gives exact orders, which the ordinary of Naples must execute without fail.

Proclus, deacon of Fermo, had already of his own accord erected a monastery on the Gressian property, and he now desired to dedicate it to St. Sabinus, martyr. For this purpose he had ap-plied to St. Gregory, who in turn wrote to Passivus, bishop of Fer-mo, that he should consecrate the new oratory after the dowry of the monastery had been legally assured (book 13, n. 16).

The relics of St. Leontius, patron of a monastery not far from Rome, had been stolen from Abbot Opportunus. As the monastic church could not be without relics of its patron, Opportunus ap-pealed to the Pope. He in turn quickly gave orders to Peter, bishop and apostolic visitator of Brindisi, to send the abbot the relics re-quested from the martyr's tomb in that place (book 6, n. 62).

At Naples Theodosius, abbot of St. Martin, had applied to the Pope to have a new monastery consecrated in honor of St. Peter and St. Michael. The monastery had been erected by his predecessor in a stable he had inherited. Gregory wrote back at once to the local bishop, Fortunatus, enjoining him at the request of the abbot to "go without trouble to the aforesaid place, when he asks, ready to celebrate the solemnities of the dedication." Note that the monastery is at Naples, the one who must consecrate it is the local bishop, but the one who must grant the authorization is the Pope. Moreover, to provide for the officiating in the sanctuary, the Pontiff orders that the priests of the church of Naples are to celebrate the Mass; in such a way, however, that through this fact neither the bishop nor the priests arrogate to themselves any new right over the new monastery praeter diligentiam disciplinae (book 5, n. 37); except, that is, vigilance over the monastic discipline, which was and remained, even a century after St. Benedict, in the competence of the bishops.

Commonly, the dedication of a church or an oratory was an event of such celebrity that it brought to the place a great concourse of clergy and laity. It could happen, however, that a very poor monastery would not be in a position to afford such extraordinary expenses. On this subject we have a letter of Gregory to the subdeacon Peter, rector of the patrimony of the Roman church in Abruzzo. One Abbot Marinianus wanted the oratory of his monastery, dedicated to the Mother of God, to be consecrated the following August. He was short of funds, however. Gregory was informed of this; so the Pontiff wrote immediately to his agent, the subdeacon Peter, that he should pay the expenses of the feast: "In as much as the poverty of the house requires it . . . we desire you to give for celebrating the dedication, to be distributed to the poor, ten golden solidi, thirty amphorae of wine, two hundred lambs, two tuns of oil, twelve sheep and a hundred chickens" (book 1, n. 56).

How interesting it would be if we could find a similar pontifical document referring to the consecration of the Cassinese oratories!

It seems that the bishop returned annually to celebrate the Mass in these monastic chapels on the anniversary day of the consecration and on the feast of the titular saint. "If on the day of the saint's anniversary, or of the dedication, of the aforesaid monastery the bishop should come there for celebrating the sacred solemnities of Mass . . ." (book 7, n. 12).

The Bishops and the Monasteries

Once a monastery had the honor of having its own oratory duly consecrated, it was no longer in the choice of the diocesan bishop to prevent the celebration of Mass there.

Bishop John of Orvieto, for example, tried to do just that; but it was an evil day for him! He received such a reproof from St. Gregory as to put the idea out of his head for some time: "that you prohibit the celebration of Masses in the said monastery, and also interdict burial of the dead there. Now, if this is so, we exhort you to desist from such inhumanity" (book 1, n. 12).

Monte Cassino also had its "cemetery for the brethren" on the summit of the mount, around the shrine of St. John the Baptist. It was precisely there, in the cave under the "oracle" of Apollo, that St. Benedict prepared his own sepulcher and that of his sister Scholastica.[11]

But let us again glean as much useful information as we can from the letters of St. Gregory to illustrate still better the relations of the monks and the abbots with the episcopal or simply ecclesiastical authority in the sixth and seventh centuries.

In the Estate of Marato, the priest assigned to the spiritual care of the place would have liked to bring new fiscal customs into the monastery of St. George. St. Gregory, being informed of it, at once wrote to his cartularius Stephanus to make opposition, and not permit the usage observed during the last three years to be changed (Letters, book 2, n. 28).

In a letter to Castorius, bishop of Rimini (book 2, n. 41), the holy Pontiff lays a sort of juridical foundation for what was subsequently called the exemption of the monasteries from the will of the bishop. I say "will" (arbitrio) intentionally, and not yet pastoral authority; for at that time no one yet thought of withdrawing the monasteries from the immediate jurisdiction of their own bishop and shepherd, to make them depend instead on their own internal superiors in the name of the distant Apostolic See.

The Pope therefore forbids that: 1) in case of a vacancy in the abbatial chair, the monastic patrimony be inventoried for the benefit of the episcopal church;

2) at the election by the monastic community, the bishop prefer and ordain as abbot his own candidate instead;

3) solemn Masses be celebrated by the bishop in the monastic oratory, with public attendance even of women;

4) against the abbot's wishes, the bishop take a monk away from the monastery to promote him to sacred orders or to designate him as superior of another community.

Bishops are likewise forbidden to erect baptistries in the monastic chapels. Among others, one of them had been erected in the diocese of Taormina; but Gregory the Great, hearing of the fact, immediately gave orders to Bishop Secundinus that he should fill up the basin of the baptistry at once, construct an altar over it and then consecrate the altar (Letters, book 3, n. 59).

In those times of invasions and wars it sometimes happened

that priests and deacons would simultaneously obtain charge of churches and of monasteries. Perhaps at Casinum also St. Benedict had found himself in a position not unlike that, being constrained to be both abbot and missionary to the neighboring peasants newly converted to the faith. St. Gregory, however, observes that such a double charge becomes practically incompatible, and for that reason in a letter to Bishop Maximianus of Syracuse he forbids it absolutely (book 4, letter 11).

The ordination of the new abbot at that time involved the celebration of Mass by the bishop, with a ceremony of inauguration or of investiture. Such an episcopal rite was required even on the hypothesis that the nomination of the abbot had been made directly by the Pope (book 11, n. 48). In such a case the Apostolic See would nominate, but would then restore the one chosen to the local diocesan authority for the ritual blessing and for the investiture.

St. Benedict and the Diocesan Authority

Returning now to the first question, under what bishop St. Benedict lived at Subiaco as well as at Monte Cassino, I must observe at once that, while the canon law then in force put both monasteries and monks in general under the vigilance of the diocesan bishop — a vigilance limited by the restrictions recorded above — still through want of documents we do not know anything about the necessary relations which must have held between the monasteries of Subiaco and Cassino and the episcopal authority. I say that there must necessarily have been relations there; but in the particular case we do not possess the documentation of them.

From the Letters of St. Gregory, however, another possibility arises. Sometimes the monasteries appear to be immediately dependent on the Holy See, so that the local bishop can consecrate neither priest nor altar there without the Pope's permission. Sometimes such immediate dependence on the Roman See had been determined by the fact that the place on which the monastery was built found itself already in the dominion of the Holy See.

Concerning Equitius, abbot of numerous monasteries in Abruzzo, "father of many monasteries in the same province", Gregory himself attests that he was living under the direct jurisdiction of the Pope: "and you have not received permission to preach from the Roman Pontiff, under whom you live" (Dialogs, book 1, ch. 4); so that the defensor Julianus was sent to bring him to Rome for a severe canonical process.

Did St. Benedict at Monte Cassino have Constantius of Aquino for bishop? Was he dependent rather on the metropolitan of Capua? Or was he immediately subject to the Apostolic See? He certainly had relations with Bishop Constantius; in so much as the latter once sent to him to be cured a cleric possessed by a devil (Dialogs, book 2, ch. 16), for whom various pilgrimages made to the tombs of martyrs had proved fruitless.

Aquino, governed at that time by Constantius, must have been reduced to quite a small diocese; so that when the bishop was about to die, he prophesied that he would actually be succeeded by a muleteer, and the latter by a weaver, but then ruin would come. And so indeed it happened. Constantius ruled the church of Aquino up to the year 573. But as St. Gregory reports, after the rapid succession of the two bishops foretold, Andrew and Jovinus, at the invasion of the Lombards into the territory of the Campania everything was destroyed and dispersed; so that there was no longer anyone at Aquino to elect a new bishop or anyone to be elected.

To this Constantius is directed a letter, very likely from Bishop Victor of Capua, to accompany a Lectionary drawn up by him at

Constantius' request. The concern is with a real liturgical lectionary, with the scriptural pericopes assigned to the various feasts of the yearly cycle. In Lent, however, according to the Milanese custom already attested to by St. Ambrose, there are added scriptural extracts of a moral nature for the instruction of the catechumens (P. L., vol. 30, cols. 501-504; Revue Bénédictine, VII, pp. 416-423, 1890).

This episcopal initiative towards liturgical unity by means of an identical scriptural lectionary, in the zone comprising Aquino and Capua with Monte Cassino in the middle, is very significant and interesting. If Constantius and Victor were thinking of liturgical unity, would they not have thought also of monastic disciplinary unity by means of a common Rule for Monks?

Of the relations of St. Benedict with the see of Capua we know only the episode when the Patriarch in ecstasy beheld the happy passing of Bishop Germanus, who was ascending to heaven in the form of a fiery ball. The event happened near the end of 540. In that same night St. Benedict hastened to dispatch a messenger to Cassino and from there to Capua to get information about Germanus. If the concern had been simply to verify a revelation, there was surely no need of all that nocturnal haste and that toil over mountains and across the plain! There were 80 miles to run at full gallop! St. Benedict's order indicates that there must have been other reasons which obliged him to interest himself in the affairs of Capua and of the holy death of his metropolitan. There would be the funeral, when it was the liturgical custom for the bishops and clergy to gather from the neighboring dioceses to render the last honors to the deceased metropolitan. The Apostle of the Cassinese could not be missing.

St. Benedict and the Apostolic See

On the other hand, we know hardly anything of the relations of St. Benedict with Rome and with the Apostolic See.

Is it possible that the holy Patriarch, once he had abandoned house, parents and the comforts of a respectable life in the Eternal City in his youth, would not then have had any more relations with Rome?

St. Gregory himself insinuates to us that there certainly must have been relations with the Romans at Subiaco as well as at Monte Cassino. The Pontiff tells how he learned the details of the life of the solitary of Monte Marsico named Martin, including his relations with St. Benedict: "I myself learned many things both from my predecessor Pope Pelagius of blessed memory and from other very religious men" (Dialogs, book 3, ch. 16). Papal Rome, therefore, was not without interest in the monastic movement promoted by St. Benedict in the Campania. The Patriarch of monasticism must hardly have reached the years of maturity when the Simbruini valley was already a whole garden of little monasteries, full of the most beautiful buds of every virtue. St. Gregory in his works sometimes mentions the diocese of Tivoli, under which Subiaco stood, its parishes, its bishops and its pastors.

* * *

In book 3 of the Dialogs, chapter 35, the story is told of Bishop Floridus, whose holiness and sincerity, Gregory adds, is well known also to the deacon Peter. This Tiburtine bishop seems to have been in particular favor with the Pontiff; so that the Pope once wanted to detain him for a few days in the infirmary of the patriarch's residence, that he might enjoy his company together with that of another holy priest of his diocese whose acquaintance the Pontiff wanted to make.

The vicissitudes of the parish of St. Peter of Affile were followed in the Lateran, where knowledge was had also of the renowned priest Florentius, pastor of the parish next to St. Benedict's monastery.

The biographer Pontiff shows that he also knows the parish of that other good priest who on Easter day divided his lunch with the hermit of Subiaco, and he reports that the parish was rather far away.

In short, the 40 miles which divided Subiaco from the City were not then so much as to prevent a whole series of ecclesiastical relations between the Tiburtine diocese and the Apostolic See.

In an atmosphere of favor and of veneration, especially after the first prodigies worked, St. Benedict easily became the most important personage of the region.

The fame of such a supernatural environment and, still more, the magnetism of the young Wonder-Worker could not fail to reach Rome; and "it was about this time", St. Gregory says, "that pious noblemen from Rome first came to visit the Saint and left their sons with him to be schooled in the service of God. Thus Euthicius brought his son Maurus, and the senator Tertullus, Placid, both very promising boys" (Dialogs, book 2, ch. 3).

It should be noted from the Gregorian biography that these are not just visits of no special significance; it is the authorities of Rome themselves, "pious noblemen from Rome", who are entering into association with St. Benedict.

In the canon law of the time this consecration of children to the monastic life through the will of the parents was permitted, and St. Benedict even codified the conditions of it in a special chapter of the Rule, "On the Sons of Nobles and of the Poor Who Are Offered" (ch. 59).[12]

The significant fact for us at the moment is that St. Gregory mentions the very aristocracy of Rome as beginning to frequent Subiaco to hear the word of the Patriarch, and moreover developing such devotion towards him as to want to consecrate their own offspring to God through his hands.

This movement of enthusiasm aroused in Rome by the fame of St. Benedict's prodigies was not a thing that could be accomplished in a day. St. Gregory is speaking of a concourse of Roman nobility. Here, then, is a brief but very important hint for the history of St. Benedict's relations with Rome.

In the Rule there is another allusion to the liturgical customs of the Roman church. It is where St. Benedict, in describing the Morning Office, desires that the canticles to be sung every day be those which are said also at Rome: "But on the other days let there be a canticle from the Prophets, each on its own day as chanted by the Roman church" (ch. 13).

What the Benedictine "Cursus" Owes to Rome

It will be worth while to shed some light on this subject. As St. Benedict has left us in the Rule an outline of a monastic penitential, so for the divine Office he has described a true and proper cursus which medieval posterity promptly named the Cursus Sancti Benedicti.

But well into the sixth century, when canon law had attained such great development, we should expect that only a bishop or, still better, the Pope, could have traced a liturgical cursus on his own authority. It is hard to explain how one who was neither Pope nor bishop could do such a thing almost at the gates of Rome.

The fact remains, however, that the Rule does describe a cursus of the divine Office, in which we can distinguish with a high degree of precision between what is due to the holy Patriarch's free initiative and what he himself owed instead to the ancient liturgical tradition. St. Benedict appeals directly to the ancient usage in arranging the psalms of the Morning Office: "After that let two other psalms be said according to custom, namely: on Monday", etc. (ch. 13). This "custom" is undoubtedly the Roman, which will be mentioned a few lines farther on.

The arrangement of the sanctoral or festival Office also goes out of the ordinary cursus of the monastic psalmody and is therefore regulated according to the prevailing liturgical custom: "except that the psalms, the antiphons and the lessons belonging to the particular day are to be said" (ch. 14). St. Benedict is here referring to a "sanctoral" already known and consecrated by ecclesiastical tradition, in which the various feasts had special psalms, antiphons and lessons.

When the Rule, as in the present case, refers to tradition, of what tradition is it speaking? There is not even a possibility of writing about the Cassinese tradition, because the foundation was still too recent, nor was Monte Cassino an episcopal church, which might give it authority in the matter. There remains, therefore, the local tradition of the metropolitan church of Capua, to which the lectionary dedicated to Constantius of Aquino bears witness; or, better, that of the Apostolic See, to which the Saint expressly refers, at least for the morning canticles. We lack many terms of comparison to institute a comparative study on the divine Office in the various churches of the sixth century.

After the manner of the Ambrosians, St. Benedict admits the singing of a hymn for each canonical Hour. But he quickly departs from the Milanese usage in excluding, with Rome, the Office of the Lucernare in favor of Vespers, and in wanting the psalter to be recited in its entirety every week, and not merely every fifteen days, as is still done today among the Ambrosians.[13]

"For those monks show themselves too lazy in the service to which they are vowed, who chant less than the psalter with the customary canticles in the course of a week" (ch. 18). If I understand correctly, trying to read the Patriarch's thought between the lines also, the situation was as follows:

There existed already a liturgical tradition, regarded as untouchable and common to the various episcopal churches of the region, which comprised the daily Office of dawn and of evening, as well as that for the great solemnities of the Lord and of the martyrs. To this customary daily and festival cursus monastic piety used to add another heavy schedule of psalms, distributed among the different hours of the day and the various days of the week. It is in this second rich field, still open to private initiative, that St. Benedict's liturgical genius is exercised in distributing the psalter throughout the circle of seven days, but recognizing at the same time an equal liberty of distribution for other abbots.

Obviously the concern was simply with monastic piety. The psalter at that time had been adopted as the exclusive manual of ecclesiastical prayer. Let an example suffice on the subject.

Up to the time of St. Charles the Milanese church preserved intact its original rite for the great vigils of its martyrs. On those solemn occasions the psalter was divided into three sections of fifty psalms each. At night, in the basilica of the martyr, clergy and people inserted a lesson with its responsory at every half-hundred psalms. When the psalter was completed, finally the Mass of the feast followed.

68

Identical seems to have been the Roman rite described by the biographer of Pope Celestine I on the occasion of the great vigils at the basilicas of the martyrs. This Pontiff desired that before the stational Mass, the psalter be recited with the whole hundred and fifty psalms.

That, however, was simply an extraordinary rite which was performed only a few times a year. This rite the monastic piety of the sixth century had so modified as to establish beyond question the principle, "Those monks show themselves too lazy in the service to which they are vowed, who chant less than the psalter with the customary canticles in the course of a week" (ch. 18).

Considering this well defined liturgical condition; keeping in mind chapter 14, where St. Benedict in treating "How the Night Office Is to Be Said on the Feasts of the Saints" refers to the liturgical tradition which was so obvious that it did not even occur to him to name it; adverting moreover to the Lectionarius Comes already mentioned which Constantius of Aquino caused to be drawn up by his own metropolitan Victor of Capua; does anyone now imagine that it would ever have been possible for St. Benedict to create a liturgy or a monastic cursus of his own genius and impose the observance of it on the monks of the various monasteries!

No. He must simply have followed the tradition of the region, and the indication "as chanted by the Roman church" justifies the hypothesis that this very tradition of the Campania Felix was identical with that of the mother church of Rome.

St. Benedict's hymnal, which he constantly qualifies with the name of "Ambrosian" (ch. 9, 12, 13, 17), is somewhat surprising. A medieval tradition would have it that hymns were originally excluded from the Roman cursus. If so, St. Benedict would have derived them not from Rome but from Milan, perhaps by way of Capua, where St. Ambrose also sat at Council.

But the knowledge with regard to Rome is anything but certain. In fact, Paulinus in the life of St. Ambrose attests, "At this time the antiphons, hymns and vigils first began to be celebrated in the Milanese church. The devotion of this celebration remains to the present day, not only in that church but throughout all the churches of the West" (ch. 13).

The knowledge of this widespread adoption of the Ambrosian hymns is confirmed for us, moreover, not only by the various quotations of St. Augustine, Cassiodorus and St. Ildephonse, but even by the Roman synod of August, 430, where Pope Celestine argues against Nestorius, quoting precisely the Nativity hymn of St. Ambrose! "I recall that on the Nativity of our Lord Jesus Christ, Ambrose of blessed memory made all the people sing with one voice Veni, Redemptor gentium. He did not say, 'Such a birth befits man', did he?" The Pope is speaking about it as of a thing already familiar to all.

Cassiodorus confirms the same thing for us: "Consider also in the hymn of the holy bishop and confessor Ambrose, which the Church sings on the Lord's Nativity throughout Italy and Gaul: 'He goes forth from His bridal chamber' " (Epistola ad Iohannem Diaconum).

We can establish other derivations of the so-called Benedictine cursus from the ancient liturgical tradition. For example, in the Night Office for feasts, after the traditional twelve psalms, the Patriarch of Cassino adds a third nocturn with the recitation of "three canticles from the book of the Prophets", according to the ancient tradition of the East, still preserved at Milan.

As is seen, for the cursus also St. Benedict had to remain

faithful to the liturgical tradition, limiting himself merely to the distribution of the psalter through the week.

Those for Whom the "Rule" Is Intended

But the Rule of St. Benedict gives rise to another question of still greater importance. In the first place, to whom is the Rule itself directed? To the Cassinese community and to the monasteries at that time dependent on it, or in general to all monasteries whatsoever, in the most diverse territories and climates?

There can be no doubt about the answer. What up to that time had constituted the weakness of the monastic institute and threatened to compromise its existence was the fluctuation of its ascetical traditions and the lack of a true and proper legislative code binding on abbots and monks universally.

If monasticism was to emerge from that primitive period of ascetical particularism and become, in the hidden designs of Providence, a true Catholic institution in the hands of the hierarchy, two conditions were necessary: that a universal authority, such as the papacy, take the initiative in giving Latin monachism unity of ascetical direction and of monastic discipline; and further, that a common Rule for Monks be promulgated, with a real obligatory character in the face of the episcopal authority as well as of the abbots and monks themselves.

These two conditions are clearly indicated in the Rule of St. Benedict.

It goes out of the limited territory of the Campania Felix and considers the monasteries of northern Italy, where the climate is more rugged. The author, however, is writing in a place of moderate climate, between the northern regions and Roman Africa or Sicily: "Let clothing be given to the brethren according to the nature of the place in which they dwell and its climate; for in cold

regions more will be needed, and in warm regions less. . . . We
believe, however, that in ordinary (mediocribus) places the following dress is sufficient", etc. (ch. 55). It is precisely in those
mediocribus locis, that is in those temperate climates, such as
central Italy, that the beans and other "fresh vegetables" granted
as a third dish in chapter 39 of the Rule are eaten raw.

In chapter 40, "On the Measure of Drink", the Lawgiver likewise takes account of the various local requirements. In warm regions, or when the life is very fatiguing, the need of wine is greater. There may be countries, however, in which wine is not found
at all, as in the northern countries.

All these diverse conditions the Patriarch of Cassino keeps in
mind while he is writing the Rule, and he gives different norms for
the diverse conditions of place, climate and life of the monks: "If
the circumstances of the place, or the work, or the heat of summer
require a greater measure, the superior shall use his judgment in
the matter . . . But where the circumstances of the place are such
that not even the measure prescribed above can be supplied, but
much less or none at all, let those who live there bless God."

Obviously he intended the Rule to hold as a general norm of
monastic life in different regions.

* * *

But what juridical value has this single Rule which is meant to
extend to all monasteries in general? Is it merely a set of sugges-
tions? Is it perhaps a manual written for the convenience of the
abbots, to render the grave charge of the command easier and more
secure for them? Is it a compendium of the ascetical life, drawn
up in the spirit of the Rule of St. Basil, the Conferences and Insti-

tutes of Cassian, mirrors of perfection proposed to all cenobites, but with a private character and without real juridical binding force?

Quite to the contrary. The Rule is "holy". It is a law for the abbots as much as for the monks, which no one is allowed to transgress.

From the very beginning, the one who is writing and speaking takes the tone and authority of the lawgiver, who is not arguing or seeking to convince, but unquestionably teaching and commanding. "And so we are going to establish a school for the service of the Lord. In founding it we hope to introduce nothing harsh or burdensome." The independence of the abbots, each of whom was the living rule of his monastery, has had its day. From now on, all must subject themselves to one common Rule for Monks, commencing with the abbots.

"In all things, therefore, let all follow the Rule as guide, and let no one be so rash as to deviate from it.

"At the same time, the abbot himself should do all things in the fear of God and in observance of the Rule" (ch. 3).

"If a brother . . . habitually transgressing the Holy Rule in any point . . ." (ch. 23).

"The authority of the Rule should also provide for them" (ch. 37).

"But let him understand that, according to the law of the Rule, from that day forward he may not . . . withdraw his neck from under the yoke of the Rule" (ch. 58).

"Let the abbot . . . keep this Rule in all its details" (ch. 64).

"If the prior should be proved to be a despiser of the holy Rule . . . let him be deposed from the office of prior" (ch. 65).

"We desire that this Rule be read often in the community, so that none of the brethren may excuse himself on the ground of ignorance" (ch. 66).

"Now we have written this Rule in order that by its observance in monasteries . . .

"Fulfil with the help of Christ this minimum Rule which we have written for beginners" (ch. 73).

* * *

While this Authority who imposes his <u>Rule</u> or law not just on Monte Cassino alone but on all monasteries in general — "that by its observance in monasteries" — is so condescending that he leaves many particular cases up to the discretion of the abbots, yet for other points of observance he decidedly opposes the previous customs and even puts a limit to the power of the bishops.

Here are some texts in which the Patriarch of monks defers to the judgment of the abbots.

"We strongly recommend, however, that if this distribution of the psalms is displeasing to anyone, he should arrange them otherwise, in whatever way he considers better, but taking care in any case that the psalter with its full number of a hundred and fifty psalms be chanted every week" (ch. 18).

The concession really seems to be a major one, in as much as it diminishes liturgical unity in the monasteries. But here the holy Lawgiver felt somewhat constrained. It was less difficult to change some disciplinary observance in the monasteries than to change the traditional order observed in the various churches for the divine Offices. The thing might easily have caused scandal. That was the reason for St. Benedict's concession.

"The degree of fault is estimated by the abbot's judgment" (ch. 24

"It shall lie within the abbot's discretion and power, should it be expedient, to add something to the fare. Above all things, however, over-indulgence must be avoided" (ch. 39).

"If . . . the heat of summer require a greater measure, the superior shall use his judgment in the matter" (ch. 40).

"This dinner at the sixth hour . . . the abbot's foresight shall decide on this" (ch. 41).

"This" (concerning clothing) "is to be taken into consideration, therefore, by the abbot. . . . The abbot shall see to the size of the garments" (ch. 55).

These and other texts demonstrate the easy adaptability of the Rule to the different conditions of various monasteries. But there are other texts which point to a sort of renovation of the previous monastic law, and a limitation of the very power of the bishops over the monasteries.

After having passed from the small communities of Subiaco to the larger and more populous community of Cassino, St. Benedict distinguishes two types of monastery: larger communities and communities of restricted number.

"If the community is a large one, let the psalms be sung with antiphons; but if small, let them be sung straight through" (ch. 17).

"If the community is a large one, let there be . . . appointed deans" (ch. 21).

"If the community is a large one, let helpers be given him" (the cellarer, ch. 31).

"If the community is a large one, the cellarer shall be excused from the kitchen service" (ch. 35).

Prior or Deans?

Throughout the writings of St. Gregory we notice that the almost universal custom in Italian monasteries of the sixth and seventh centuries had provided each abbot with a prior, generally designated by the local episcopal authority, as his auxiliary and substitute. Moreover, the title praepositus is significant; for in the Roman basilicas the praepositus was the head of the local clergy, the one who presided over the administration in the Pontiff's name

St. Benedict absolutely disapproves of the dangerous system, which could easily create dualisms in the bosom of the community. Against that peril he invokes instead the great Roman axiom of governing, which advises dividing the responsibilities among the minor hierarchies, and then giving orders at the head of all: "Divide and rule."

The Patriarch of Cassino readily attributes to priors created by the bishops the evils of pride, tyranny, dualism, which create scandals in the monastery and leave souls hanging on the brink of damnation. These disadvantages are still greater "in those places where the prior is constituted by the same bishop or the same abbots who constitute the abbot himself" (ch. 65).

To get away from the abuses he wants to change the system and substitute for the prior as vice-abbot the institution of deans, derived from the old Pachomian monachism. Each dean, under the overall direction of the abbot, would have been like a corporal in charge of his own group of monks; and the resulting advantage would have been that "with the duties being shared by several, no one person will become proud" (ch. 65).

There was no argument about this principle of government, an essentially Roman one which divided the competences and responsibilities among the minor hierarchies and reserved to the chief the office of commanding; except that St. Benedict here hit against two rocks which stood so firm that he had to yield.

There was first the monastic custom almost universal in Italy which joined the prior to the abbot. Moreover, the appointment of the prior was not left completely to the personal initiative of the monastic superior. The election of the prior represented a juridical institution which entered into the competence of the diocesan bishop and often also of the regional assembly of abbots. It could be supposed from the very beginning that these persons would not be so readily disposed to abdicate their peaceful right and adapt themselves to the radical reform which the abbot of Monte Cassino wanted to introduce.

St. Benedict had well foreseen the opposition and the difficulty his innovation would encounter; so that in certain cases he tolerates the choice of a prior: "But if the circumstances of the place require it, or if the community asks for it with reason and with humility, and the abbot judges it to be expedient, let the abbot himself constitute as his prior whomsoever he shall choose with the counsel of God-fearing brethren."

According to the Cassinese Lawgiver, therefore, there should be no prior, but only deans. But if the naming of a prior should seem more opportune, let there be no interference by the bishop or by the assembly of abbots of the region, but let it be the abbot of the monastery himself who freely chooses the prior who meets with his approval.

The reform is rather daring. It is true that the scandals it is intended to eliminate are not infrequent — "It happens all too often" — nor slight — "they foster scandals and cause dissensions". It is true that St. Benedict here uses exceptionally strong language, actually calling the previous system absurd: "What an absurd procedure this is can easily be seen." It is true that he makes all the responsibility for it fall on the bishop and the abbots who uphold it:

"The guilt for this dangerous state of affairs rests on the heads of those whose action brought about such disorder."

Frankly, such strong language would be perfectly in its place in the vigorous letters of St. Gregory the Great or of some other Pope; but it is almost incomprehensible under the meek pen of the abbot of Monte Cassino, even in so far as he is Saint and Wonder-Worker. I should prefer almost to believe that this chapter of the Rule has preserved for us some quotations from a lost papal document about the election of priors in the monasteries of Italy.

The Historical Tradition in Favor of Priors

The fact remains, then, that, despite the two chapters of the Rule in which the system of deans is defended — chapters 21 and 65 — in the Italian monasteries of the first centuries of the Middle Ages we find no deans at all. Instead we observe everywhere that at the abbot's side there was a prior to act as his deputy. Thus it was before St. Benedict, and thus it continued after him, with rare exceptions.

I cite some examples treated by St. Gregory in his Dialogs. St. Nonnosus was prior of the monastery on Mount Soracte (book 1, ch. 7); Libertinus and Felix Corvus were priors successively in the monastery of Funda (book 1, ch. 2, 3). St. Benedict himself in founding a monastery at Terracina names its abbot and its prior (book 2, ch. 22). St. Gregory later records the prior of his monastery of St. Andrew on the Clivus Scauri, on the Caelian hill (book 4, ch. 55).

Gleaning in the Letters of St. Gregory, we find some really interesting cases. To Abbot John (perhaps of St. Lucy in Syracuse) St. Gregory had already assigned a good monk to help him restore the fortunes of that monastery, the community having lapsed seriously from the old discipline. Some time later the abbot asked the Pope for permission actually to name him prior. St. Gregory replied, "Your Love asks that Brother Boniface may be ordained prior by you in your monastery; and I wonder indeed why this was not done before. You should have ordained him as soon as I had given him to you" (book 3, n. 3).

In another letter, to Bishop Victor of Palermo, St. Gregory treats of a similar case. He had detained Abbot Gregory of St. Theodore at Rome for a long penance, because through negligence he had let the souls of so many of his monks go to hell. Finally pardoning him, he restored him to his charge, but at the same time ordered Urbicus, prior of St. Andrew on the Caelian hill, to assign him some good monk of his for the office of prior, adding, "that what is neglected through the carelessness of Gregory may be preserved through the solicitude of the other" (book 5, letter 6). How far we are from the monarchical concept of the abbot ruling the community alone with no help but that of the deans!

On another occasion it was reported to Gregory that at Rimini Abbot Agnellus was doing everything by himself, not tolerating the aid of any prior. St. Gregory disapproves such a system of centralization, and desires that a good prior be named at once (book 7, letter 10).

Again, the Pope sends the monk Barbatianus to Naples invested with the powers of prior, with the intention of developing him into a worthy abbot for the monastery erected there. The bishop of the city, Fortunatus, will keep him on probation, therefore. After the lapse of some time he will finally promote him to the abbatial dignity (book 9, letter 91).

The probation, however, turned out less happily. The bishop was in too much of a hurry to promote him; so that Barbatianus, once he had become a prelate, did not live up to the Pope's expectations. One time, among other things, he admitted to monastic profession one who had not even passed a short time of probation or, as it is called, of novitiate. There happened inevitably what could easily have been foreseen. The newly professed soon ran away from the cloister. Hence Gregory writes resentfully to the bishop of Naples, forbidding that henceforth anyone from that place be admitted to the monastic vows without having passed a good two years of novitiate! As to accepting the vocations of soldiers, the Pope reserves permission to himself (book 10, n. 24). This is something other than the abbot described in the Rule, who is "lord" and "abbot" in his monastery!

On another occasion Gregory the Great orders Bishop Victor (perhaps of Palermo) to betake himself to the monastery of Lucca, celebrate Mass and ordain a priest named Domitius abbot, while the Pope was directly choosing as prior the monk Lucifer, already cellarer of the community (book 11, n. 48).

In conclusion, the system of monastic deans so strongly defended by St. Benedict, however sporadic and fragmentary be the documents which remain to us of monastic Italy of the sixth century, seems not to have met with success. Even after the propagation of the Rule at Rome and in Gaul, the one who helps the abbot in the government of the monastery is regularly the prior; and he, moreover, is chosen not just exclusively by the abbot but by either the Pope or the bishop of the place.

* * *

Another point on which the prescription of St. Benedict is soon overruled by a different pontifical statute is the duration of the no-

vitiate. According to the Patriarch of Cassino, the monastic probation lasts an entire year, and this space of time seems quite long
to him (Rule, ch. 58: "during that prolonged deliberation"). For St.
Gregory, on the other hand, the novitiate must be prolonged a good
two years, and for soldiers the consent of the holy See is an absolute prerequisite (book 10, n. 24): "and by no means let them ven-
ture to tonsure those whom they may have received for monastic
profession before they have completed two years in monastic life."

The Priests in the Monasteries

Another point of the Benedictine Rule which encountered opposition in the ecclesiastical law of the sixth century was the ordination of the priests in the service of the monastery.

St. Benedict in the Rule had assigned to the abbot the right of
choosing the monks to be candidates for the priesthood. "If an abbot
desire to have a priest or a deacon ordained for his monastery, let
him choose one of his monks who is worthy to exercise the priestly
office" (ch. 62). We observe instead in St. Gregory's Letters something which considerably weakens the unappealable decision of the
abbot.

Abbot Urbicus of Palermo in the name of his community had ap-
pealed to the Pontiff to have a priest for the religious service of
the monastery. The Pope therefore wrote to the diocesan Bishop
Victor, ordering him to go to the place, "that he should consecrate
. . . the one who shall have been elected for this ministry from
that community" (book 6, n. 42). The monks as well as the abbot
have a say in the election of their priest.

Also in the "Precoritan" monastery of Palermo there is want
of a priest, and the monks have therefore written about it to the
Pope. Gregory again writes to Bishop Victor that "he should ordain

as priest . . . the one whom they have unanimously chosen for themselves from their community in the aforesaid monastery" (book 9, n. 92). The abbot is not mentioned at all; but, according to the custom of the time, it is the community which unanimously elects and makes the canonical request. In treating of monks, subjects of privileged canonical right, the local bishop does nothing but control the regularity of the election and then consecrate the new priest — "the community which asks to have him ordained for them" — giving him charge of fulfilling the divine services in the monastery's church, as the Pope had ordered.

The new priest, however, ordained though he be, must no longer be considered at the disposal of the bishop for the spiritual needs of the diocese. Gregory expressly declares this to the one who ordains. Then as the canonical customs of the time might have been able to render this provision vain, the Pope interposes his pontifical authority: "Let it be established by our authority also that he observe[14] neither in the church nor in any other place, but that he stay there perpetually."

The prescriptions of St. Benedict's Rule, without any papal interposition, are more absolute and do not take into due account the juridical circumstances regarding the sacred ordinations of the monks. To these Gregory himself sometimes yields; as, for instance, when he did consecrate as deacon a monk presented to him by Abbot Elias of Isauria, but kept him at Rome, giving as reason the bond of the sacred ordination (book 5, n. 38). But this confirms our suspicion that the Lawgiver of Cassino is the agent for determining a plan of juridical reform, not so much on his own account, but rather for the Holy See or for his own metropolitan, who perhaps had given him an express commission to do so.

The two chapters of the Rule, chapter 60, "On Priests Who May Wish to Live in the Monastery", and chapter 62, "On the Priests of the Monastery", interpenetrate each other and to some extent repeat each other; and it is not clear how in the official editing of the Rule they have been separated by chapter 61, which concerns pilgrim monks rather than priests.

But there is some obscurity; for it is hard to understand how the first place after the abbot is assigned to the priest who comes to be made a monk; to the cleric is promised a middle place; and on the other hand, the monk ordained priest there in the monastery itself is told bluntly: you remain in the place of your entrance into the monastery, except when you are ministering at the altar! St. Benedict returns insistently to this point in both chapters, with almost the same words: "Let him always keep the place he received on entering the monastery, except in his duties at the altar" (ch. 62). But the doubt persists. For greater clarity, let us here look over the conditions laid down for the priest in the two different chapters:

Chapter 60

"On Priests Who May Wish to Live in the Monastery."

"It shall be granted him to stand next after the abbot."

"If any clerics . . . should wish to join the monastery, let them be placed in a middle rank."

"If his presence in the

Chapter 62

"On the Priests of the Monastery".

"Let him always keep the place he received on entering the monastery."

monastery is due to his ordination or some other reason
(si forte ordinationis, aut ali-
cujus rei causa fuerit in monasterio), let him expect the
rank due him according to the
date of his entrance into the
monastery, and not the place
granted him out of reverence
for the priesthood."

Between the two chapters there is not really any discord; but
they are different ways of conceiving two similar situations. The
first situation is that of those already belonging to the clergy who
want to be received among the monks. For these, in homage to
their sacred character, St. Benedict shows special respect: the
priests will walk immediately after the abbot and a suitable place
will be assigned to the other clerics of lower rank. On the other
hand, when the concern is with the elevation to the priesthood of a
monk of the community, as an ordinary rule he does not change his
place, but keeps his rank of seniority in the community, except in
the service of the altar or in special cases of advancement for the
particular merit of his holy life.

Then there is a sort of third category, which is harder to
identify. It comprises those whose "presence in the monastery is
due to their ordination or some other reason", who have no privilege in the community but proceed simply in the order of seniority.
Who are these, and in what way do they differ from the other two
categories? If a suitable place is granted even to mere clerics, why
is there no special distinction for these last?

Perhaps the uncertainty can be cleared up for us by St. Gregory's Letters. At that time it was not unusual for an abbot to petition the diocesan bishop or the Roman Pontiff that a priest be ordained from the ranks of the clergy and then assigned to the celebration of the divine Offices in the monastery.

Thus we have an example with regard to the sepulchral basilica of St. Pancratius in Rome. Gregory removes it from the titular priests and assigns it instead to a community of monks under the government of Abbot Maurus. But for the celebration of the divine Mysteries the Pope establishes "that you do not fail to employ an attending (peregrinum) priest to celebrate the sacred solemnities of Mass. But he must live in your monastery and be supported by it" (book 4, n. 18). The phrasing of the apostolic chancellery "to live in the monastery" brings to mind precisely the wording used also by St. Benedict, "On Priests Who May Wish to Live in the Monastery". The concern in both cases, therefore, is not just with a priest who freely leaves his hierarchical office to become a monk, but with a priest who has been ordained for the very purpose of assignment as chaplain to a particular monastery. He will reside in the monastery, therefore, and be supported by it.

The Expulsion of Priests from the Monastery

More important juridically is the question of the expulsion from the monastery of monks elevated to the priesthood when their dissolute life makes them unworthy of staying there. St. Benedict prescribes that, after due and repeated warnings have been made to the culprit, the intervention of the bishop should be finally invoked, as "witness" of this summary procedure. If the incorrigibility still persists, then let the guilty one be expelled from the monastery: "Let even the bishop be brought in as a witness. If then he still fails to amend, and his offenses are notorious, let him be put out of the monastery" (ch. 62).

Such a procedure against a priest is very serious, and I hesitate to believe that it can proceed from the mere authority of St. Benedict, abbot of Monte Cassino, when it involves the very power of the ordained diocesan bishops and even that of the Pope.

Still less does their expulsion from the monastery square with the discipline of the time when, according to the custom, it was precisely to the monasteries that priests and deacons guilty of grave offenses were consigned to do penance.

That was just what St. Gregory the Great established for the Maltese priests and deacons in one of his letters: "Certain priests and deacons . . . let him likewise lower their rank also and assign them to monasteries where they can worthily do penance" (book 9, n. 63).

Then there is another very important letter of St. Gregory. Romanus, papal defensor of Sicily, was not hesitating to try at his tribunal the cases of the ecclesiastics of that island. But the Pope intervenes and firmly forbids his subaltern to invade the rights of the bishops: "If anyone should have a suit against any cleric, let him go to his bishop. . . . For, if each single bishop has not his own jurisdiction reserved to him, what else are We doing but confounding ecclesiastical order when We should be guarding it?" (book 11, n. 37).

Not only ecclesiastics but monks also were exempt from the tribunal of the laity and subject rather to that of the local bishop. Gregory the Great reminds Bishop Fortunatus of Naples of that fact: "We forbid . . . that either a cleric or a monk . . . of your parish be summoned by anyone, nor do we want them to be exposed to the judgment of another" (book 6, n. 11).

86

Again, the Pope orders Bishop Victor of Palermo to consecrate as priest a monk whom a certain community of that diocese
had chosen for the religious service of their own chapel. The request had been made directly to the Pontiff, who in referring the
ordination back to the diocesan bishop declares that the newly chos-
en priest — also by pontifical disposition: "by our authority also" —
can no longer be assigned either to another church or to another
ecclesiastical office (book 9, n. 92).

In a letter to Bishop Chrysanthus of Spoleto the same Pontiff
prescribes the procedure to be followed in the judging of a priest.
The _defensor_ or pontifical _procurator_ could act as public prosecut-
or, beginning by denouncing the offense to the episcopal tribunal.
If the contumacy of the ecclesiastic did not cease, there followed
the "admonition" of the bishop, after which the canonical penalty
was in order. "If . . . he find any who are insolent, the priestly
admonition having been given and, if the matter require, also im-
posing the canonical discipline, let him hasten to amend for the
future. . . . But as for a priest also . . . let your Fraternity be
zealous to admonish or reprove him for such things. And if he will
not hear you, suspend him from Communion" (book 13, n. 36).

St. Benedict's procedure is more summary; but perhaps in the
sheets left incomplete by the holy Patriarch it represents, rather
than a definitive law, the mere scheme of a penitential canon which
the Roman Pontiff would then have had to sanction in order to put
it into effect. There was no longer question of a mere abbatial
competence! The Patriarch's death and the unhappy vicissitudes of
the various Popes who succeeded one another during St. Benedict's
last years must probably have prevented this immediate ratification
on the part of the pontifical authority.

In other letters also, as in those he wrote to the _defensor_ John

when he sent him to Spain, Gregory upholds insistently the idea
that both ecclesiastics and monks should be subject to the tribunal
of the diocesan bishop, quoting in support one of Justinian's Novels
(book 13, n. 45, ch. 2).

The Election of the Abbot

With regard to the constituting of an abbot, St. Benedict stands
firm on the principle that it be exclusively for the monks to elect
him. A good many of St. Gregory's letters are documents confirm-
ing the same statute, yet reserving to the diocesan bishop either
the control over the canonical election or the investiture of the abbot
elect, which regularly took place during the episcopal celebration
of the divine Sacrifice.

In the Rule St. Benedict twice indicates a sort of control or
surveillance on the part of a regional commission of abbots:

"But if . . . those vices somehow become known to the bishop
to whose diocese the place belongs, or to the abbots or the faithful
of the vicinity, let them prevent the success of this conspiracy of
the wicked, and set a worthy steward over the house of God" (ch.
64, "On Constituting an Abbot").

"Especially does this happen in those places where the prior
is constituted by the same bishop or the same abbots who constitute the abbot himself" (ch. 65, "On the Prior of the Monastery").

There were regions, therefore, where custom reserved the
election of the new abbot or of the new prior to a sort of general
chapter of the bishop and the regional abbots.

In St. Gregory's Letters there is again some reference to this
sort of general chapter of abbots, to whom the Pontiff now attributes the task of deciding in common the questions of patrimonial
order which might happen to arise between bishops and monasteries.

"But, if any case should by chance arise as to land disputed between their churches and any monasteries, and it cannot be arranged amicably, let it be decided without avoidable delay before selected abbots and other fathers who fear God, sworn upon the most holy Gospels.

". . . If, circumstances requiring it, the abbot of a place should have questions with other abbots concerning property that has come into possession, let the matter be decided also by their counsel or judgment" (book 2, n. 41).

In case of an inappropriate choice of abbot, the bishop or the neighboring abbots, according to the text of the Benedictine Rule, could intervene to prevent it or to substitute a more suitable individual. Who was supposed to decide whether or not the choice was a happy one? It is evident that St. Benedict is referring to the law then in force, which put these abbatial elections under the control and vigilance of the episcopal authority and in some cases even under a commission of abbots of the territory.

Another letter of St. Gregory (book 3, n. 23) is equally instructive. The Pope had deposed from office Abbot Secundinus, admittedly guilty of grave faults. The community then "petitions" for one Theodosius as abbot. The Pontiff therefore writes to his subdeacon Peter, assigned to the administration of the pontifical patrimony in Campania, to appeal to the local bishop that "you have the one solemnly ordained abbot in the monastery of St. Martin whom the community itself has asked for, by him whose function (provisio) it is."

The business of the abbatial ordination evidently was not so simple, then, that it could be resolved in the family with the mere authority of the Rule. By this time canon law required frequently the intervention of the Pope, the postulatio of the chapter, the action of the pontifical Mass and finally the provisio of the local bishop, who celebrated the Mass and the inaugural rite of solemn blessing of the new abbot.

Such an episcopal rite was celebrated also for the abbesses. St. Gregory bears witness to this in writing about it to Gennarus, metropolitan of Cagliari. "The abbess was ordained solemnly by the bishop."

At Palermo a new abbot is to be constituted in the Gregorian monastery called Lucusiano. The Pontiff writes of it to Abbot Urbicus, "Having received our letters, therefore, let your Love invite our brother and fellow Bishop Victor to the Lucusian monastery, that he should celebrate solemn Mass there and ordain as abbot, by God's authority, the aforesaid Domitius" (Letters, book 11, n. 48).

Dismissal of Abbots

In book 2 of St. Gregory's Dialogs, chapter 3, regarding St. Benedict's resignation from the abbatial charge of the monastery of Vicovaro, whose monks had tried to poison him, the deacon Peter asks Gregory whether such a withdrawal was lawful. — In the Greek version Pope Zachary somewhat modifies the question, asking τίνος χάριν might such an abandonment be permitted? — The Pope observes in reply that "a superior ought to bear patiently with a community of evil men as long as it has some devout members who can benefit from his presence." When even these latter are wanting, to what end should he remain at his post? It is better in that case not to lose time, and to go and do good elsewhere.

But it does not seem possible that dismissals and withdrawal from the monastery could have been undertaken by St. Benedict without any agreement with the episcopal authority. That is precisely the juridical objection which was disturbing the deacon Peter. The abbatial charge of its nature is perpetual. Can an abbot dismiss himself on his own initiative?

In St. Gregory's Letters the case does not even occur.

On the other hand, there are several examples of abbots deposed from their office for grave faults. Sometimes, after a long penance, the former post of command was granted them again; but generally Gregory declares himself against these reinstatements. At the most, if the abbots are also priests, while the perpetual suspension from holy orders is kept in force, the penitent is granted the first place among the monks (book 5, nn. 3, 4, 7).

Juridical Effects of the Monastic Habit

In St. Gregory's biography of St. Benedict there still remain many things that need clarification in the light of the canonical and liturgical law of the time.

St. Benedict as a youth received the monastic habit from the hand of the monk Romanus. In the usage of the time, such reception of the monastic habit and of the tonsure was equivalent to a real profession, whether or not the novitiate had preceded. This juridical custom continued for some hundreds of years during the Middle Ages.

It was just such an imprudent act for which Abbot Barbatianus of Naples had to take the consequences when "he rashly tonsured a secular person without even previous probation" (book 10, letter 24).

In Sardinia there had happened a case similar to that of the monk Romanus. A certain devota named Pomponiana had gathered a community of girls in her own house and had even conferred the religious habit on them by her own authority. Was such a profession valid? Gregory decides that they should not be molested: "Further, as to her girls whom the aforesaid Pomponiana converted in the monastery and clothed in religious dress, you must by no means let them be withdrawn from her or disquieted" (book 14, n. 2).

In Sardinia, moreover, curious things happened! A certain abbess named Sirica, against all the rules, had presumed to make a will and to leave her property to her own heirs. Was such an act valid? In favor of an affirmative answer was the observation that the late abbess to the very day of her death had always refused to assume the monastic habit, but had worn those other matronal clothes which in that country used to distinguish the former wives of priests after their vow of continence. Gregory had the case minutely studied at Rome. In the end his theologians observed that the solemn investiture of the abbess by the bishop's hand and her perseverance in the office were equivalent to an implicit monastic profession. The circumstance of her never having worn the habit did point to excessive indulgence on the bishop's part, but was not such as to render doubtful her real profession of the monastic life (book 9, n. 7).

The case of Abbot Probus, seized suddenly in the Lateran and created abbot without ever having been a monk nor having been able to dispose of his property through a will, reveals an identical juridical situation. The monastic profession was implicit.

St. Gregory I and the "Rule"

The problem has often been discussed whether St. Gregory cites the Benedictine code in any other document except the Dialogs, book 2, chapter 36, where among the prodigies achieved by the Patriarch of Cassino he mentions his Rule.

The places adduced as citations from St. Benedict are very doubtful.

Letters, book 11, n. 48. During a journey two monks quarrel because one wants the other to divide part of a _eulogia_ with him. ". . . Your Love could have known from what great bitterness of heart[15] this resulted if you had wanted to know the rule for monks." Here perhaps "the rule" stands simply for observance, as in the same document a few lines earlier: "From this I see how dissolute is the rule of the monastery."

Elsewhere St. Gregory has words so strong against the vice of property among the monks that they remind us of those of the _Rule_.

RULE OF ST. BENEDICT (ch. 33, 55).

"This vice especially is to be cut out of the monastery by the roots. . . . But if anyone is caught indulging in this most wicked vice, let him be admonished."

"The beds, moreover, are to be examined frequently by the abbot, to see if any private property be found in them. . . . And in order that this vice . . . may be cut out by the roots . . ."

(Chapter 50).

"On Brethren Who . . .

ST. GREGORY (book 12, n. 24).

"For I have learned how this same Constantius seeks to possess property of his own; and this is the strongest evidence that he has not the heart of a monk. . . . Take care . . . that he suppress emphatically the possession of property of their own by four or five of the monks of the monastery . . . and make haste to cleanse this monastery from such a plague; since, if private property is held there by monks, it will not be possible for either concord or charity to continue in that congregation."

". . . And I have learned further that he presumed to go

93

Are on a Journey." alone, without any one of his brethren with him, to a monastery that is situated in the province of Picenum. From this conduct of his we know that he who walks without a witness is not living right: and how can he maintain the rule for others when he does not know how to maintain it for himself?"

This chapter of the Rule is always in the plural; while the following chapter, where the concern is with short absences from the monastery — "and is expected to return to the monastery that same day" — is in the singular. But in chapter 12 of book 2 of the Dialogs we observe that even in this latter case the monks were at least two.

One of the things that constitute the Benedictine life is stability in one's own monastery, under the discipline of one's own abbot. "But let him understand that, according to the law of the Rule, from that day forward he may not leave the monastery nor withdraw his neck from under the yoke of the Rule" (Rule, ch. 58).

For St. Gregory such monastic stability becomes a universal norm; so much so that, having learned that in the diocese of Sorrento there were monks who at their caprice were passing from one monastery to another — "transmigrate from monastery to monastery as they please, and depart from the rule of their own abbot out of desire for a worldly life" — Gregory without hesitation orders the subdeacon Anthemius to have them arrested and restored to their own superior (book 1, n. 42).

When Augustine and his forty companions were sent by St.

Gregory to convert England to the faith, they undoubtedly introduced the Rule of St. Benedict there, as the most ancient sources testify. This St. Gregory indicates in writing to Augustine (book 11, n. 64).

"But in as much as your Fraternity, having been trained in the rules of a monastery, ought not to live apart from your clergy . . . it will be right to institute that manner of life which in the beginning of the infant Church was that of our Fathers, among whom none said that any of the things which he possessed was his own, but they had all things in common."

RULE OF ST. BENEDICT (ch. 33).
"Let all things be common to all, as it is written, and let no one say or assume that anything is his own."

Then in recommending Bishop Augustine to King Edilbert, he calls him "bishop, learned in monastic Rule" (book 11, n. 66).

In chapter 12 of book 2 of the Dialogs it seems that St. Gregory has another allusion to the Rule. Here are the two texts.

DIALOGS (book 2, ch. 12).
"It was a custom of the house, strictly observed as a matter of regular discipline, that monks away on business did not take food or drink

RULE OF ST. BENEDICT (ch. 51).
"A brother who is sent out on some business and is expected to return to the monastery that same day shall not presume to eat while he is out, even if he is

95

outside the monastery." urgently requested to do so by any person whomsoever.

Another allusion:

DIALOGS (book 2, ch. 24).	RULE OF ST. BENEDICT (ch. 67).
"One time a young monk who was too attached to his parents left the monastery without asking for the abbot's blessing and went home."	". . . Let him undergo the punishment of the Rule. And let him be punished likewise who would presume to leave the enclosure of the monastery and go anywhere . . . without an order from the abbot."

St. Benedict and the "Rule"

There is a very delicate question which has been proposed to me lately.

Does the Rule for Monks represent the personal spirit of St. Benedict?

At first glance the question may seem strange and idle. If the Rule so strongly reflects the personality of the Wonder-Worker of Monte Cassino, how could it not reflect his spirit also?

And yet, in examining some penitential chapters of the Rule in which the harsh, severe and traditional spirit of the ancient monachism still prevails, it is hard to see how they can be reconciled with the new and agreeably meek spirit which unquestionably shines through the whole biography of St. Benedict.

Let me put the various texts side by side:

96

RULE (ch. 46).

"If anyone is engaged in any sort of work . . . and he commits some fault, or breaks something, or loses something . . . let him be subjected to a more severe correction."

(Ch. 51). "On Brethren Who Go Not Very Far Away."

". . . he shall not presume to eat while he is out, even if he is urgently requested to do so by any person whomsoever. . . . And if he acts otherwise, let him be excommunicated."

Ch. 54). "Whether a

DIALOGS (book 2, ch. 6).

"Having lost his implement, the Goth ran trembling to Maurus and after describing the accident told him how sorry he was for his carelessness . . . .

"Then he (Benedict) handed the tool back to the Goth and told him, 'Continue with your work now. There is no need to be upset.' "

(Ch. 12). "Some Monks Disobey the Rule by Eating Outside the Monastery."

"It was a custom of the house . . . that monks away on business did not take food or drink outside the monastery. . . . They confessed their guilt. The man of God did not hesitate to pardon them."

(Ch. 33). "Scholastica's Miracle."

". . . As darkness was setting in, they sat down to partake of food together. While they were yet sitting at the table . . . he replied, 'I must not remain outside of the monastery.' "

(Ch. 19). "A Monk Accepts

Monk Should Receive Letters or Anything Else."

"On no account shall a monk be allowed . . . Should anyone presume to act otherwise, let him undergo the discipline of the Rule."

(Ch. 5). "On Obedience."

". . . If he murmurs, not necessarily with his lips but simply in his heart, then even though he fulfil the command yet his work will not be acceptable to God, who sees that his heart is murmuring. . . . He will incur the punishment due to murmurers."

(Ch. 31). ". . . The Cellarer of the Monastery . . ."

". . . He should do all things . . . in accordance with the abbot's instructions.

"Above all things let him have humility. . . . Let him have under his care all that the abbot has assigned to him, but not presume to deal

Some Handkerchiefs as a Present."

". . . The nuns presented the monk with a few handkerchiefs, which he accepted and hid away in his habit. . . . The offender instantly fell at Benedict's feet, confessed his fault and gave up the present he had received."

(Ch. 20). "The Man of God Reads a Young Monk's Proud Thoughts."

". . . Then calling the others together, he had one of them take the lamp instead, and told the murmurer to sit down by himself and be quiet."

(Ch. 28, 29). "A Glass Vessel Strikes against the Rocks without Breaking."

". . . He wanted nothing to remain in the monastery through disobedience. . . . Then he sent for the rest of the community and in their presence rebuked the disobedient monk for his pride and lack of faith.

with what he has forbidden him."

". . . He at once ended his prayer and the oil stopped flowing. Then turning to the monk who had shown himself disobedient and wanting in confidence, he urged him again to strive to grow in faith and humility."

(Ch. 30). "How Boys Are to Be Corrected."

". . . Whenever such as these are delinquent let them be subjected to severe fasts or brought to terms by harsh beatings, that they may be cured."

(Book 3, ch. 16). "On Martin the Monk of Mount Marsicus."

". . . He bound his foot with an iron chain, and fixed the other end of it to the rock. . . . When Benedict heard of this . . . he took pains to send him a message through one of his disciples: 'If you are a servant of God, let not an iron chain hold you, but the chain of Christ.' "

I could lengthen greatly this comparison of texts and deeds, but I consider it needless. For me, the St. Benedict of the Dialogs is not exactly the St. Benedict of the Rule, because in this labor of codification he had to include, as if in spite of himself, traditional canons and pedagogical and directive criterions, which were common at that time in the monastic atmosphere.

But the great, gentle soul of the Patriarch of Cassino, in practice, applied them in a very kind sense, "preferring mercy to justice", so as to merit the praise of the great Gregory: "He wrote a Rule for Monks that is remarkable for its discretion and its clarity of language" (ch. 36).

Conclusions

There would still be many other points to illustrate in the <u>Rule</u> of St. Benedict, but I do not intend to go into them. I simply wanted to insinuate two ideas:

1) That the <u>Rule for Monks</u> in the canonical jurisprudence of its time represents a work of codification so bold as to exclude absolutely the possibility of its having proceeded exclusively from a private authority like St. Benedict at Monte Cassino. The sole authority really competent to do it, and to which the legislative power belonged, if it was not that of the metropolitan of Capua, must be sought in Rome and in the Lateran.

2) For a better understanding of the <u>Rule</u>, extending even to its fine points, there is need to study it not with the ideas of our time but in relation to the historico-juridical conditions of the sixth and seventh centuries.

What has happened for St. Benedict's <u>Rule</u> is the same thing that has happened to some extent for another monk's anonymous writing, the <u>Imitation of Christ</u>. Although their authors were not preoccupied with the fortune of their books, God has made use of them to sanctify the whole world.

NOTES

[1] For the documentation see Ludwig Traube, Textgeschichte der Regula S. Benedicti, 2nd ed., pp. 30 ff.

[2] The chronology of the first Cassinese abbots is not entirely discoverable. We know, however, that at St. Benedict's death Pope Vigilius was a prisoner at Constantinople. It was only in 556 that Rome had the Pope again in the person of Pelagius I. Hence the action of Simplicius for the recognition of the Rule is explained: the long absence of the Pontiff is just over.

[3] Patrologia Latina (Paris: J.-P. Migne), vol. 67, col. 1099.

[4] Ibid., col. 1285.

[5] Ennodius, Letters 3, 10; edited by Frederic Vogel in Magni Felicis Ennodi Opera (Berlin: Weidmann, 1885, vol. A-7 of Monumenta Germaniae Historica), p. 83.

[6] The Pope's canonical terminology is to be noted. He does not say simply that St. Benedict gave the sorrowing parents of the deceased monk the Body of the Lord, but instead "the Communion of the Body of the Lord", in as much as with that Eucharistic "rite" he was readmitting the excommunicate to "Communion with him" and with the Church.

[7] By this expression St. Gregory clearly describes the ceremony. St. Benedict "gave the Communion . . . at once with his own hand", to indicate the ritual act of celebrating the Eucharist, which puts the dead one back into Communion.

[8] This priestly activity of a "continual preaching", at a time when preaching was so much the property of the bishop that it was hardly granted to priests, and in some places not granted them at all, has its counterpart in St. Gregory's remark that "not a few persons" had embraced the faith through the Saint's exhortations (ch. 19).

[9]In the age of Gregory the office of <u>defensor</u> was equivalent to a sort of <u>conservator</u> or papal delegate. A <u>defensor</u> in Sicily was summoning even ecclesiastics to his own tribunal, thus supplanting the authority of the bishops. Gordianus, father of St. Gregory I, was himself a <u>defensor</u>.

[10]Gregory's <u>Registrum</u> is a good half century later than St. Benedict; but it still represents the traditional right of the Roman Church, without anything to authorize seeing in St. Gregory's documents a general renovation of the <u>Ius Canonicum</u>, above all in the relations between the episcopate and monachism. That was not the time for making juridical changes!

[11]St. Gregory relates that St. Benedict sent his monks to transport to Monte Cassino the virginal body of his sister, there to be buried in his own tomb (<u>Dialogs</u>, book 2, ch. 34). The juridical difficulty of an invasion of the "parochial rights" can be excluded, it seems, by the circumstance that the "cell" of the consecrated virgin probably stood at the base of Monte Cassino, where since the tenth century we find a little church in honor of the saint. That <u>tricora</u> in its turn rises over the remains of former habitations.

[12]Later, St. Gregory forbade that anyone be admitted into a monastery under the age of 18 in the islands of the Tyrrhenum. But the concern is with particular precautions and not with general laws (<u>Letters</u>, book 1, n. 50).

[13]We should note, however, that the fifteen Ambrosian "decades" appear already in St. Augustine's <u>Enarrationes in Psalmos</u>, and recur also with Cassiodorus.

[14]"To observe" signifies properly to mount guard. Still today in Milan the <u>presbyter observator</u> is the canonical hebdomadary.

[15]This "bitterness of heart" recalls the "evil zeal of bitterness" of which the <u>Rule</u> speaks in chapter 72.